Designing Service
Processes to Unlock Value

Designing Service Processes to Unlock Value

Third Edition

Joy M. Field

BEP

BUSINESS EXPERT PRESS

Leader in applied, concise business books

First published in 2021 by
Business Expert Press, LLC
222 East 46th Street, New York, NY 10017
www.businessexpertpress.com

ISBN-13: 978-1-95334-926-2 (paperback)
ISBN-13: 978-1-63742-333-2 (hardcover)
ISBN-13: 978-1-95334-927-9 (e-book)

Business Expert Press Service Systems and Innovations in Business and Society Collection

Collection ISSN: 2326-2664 (print)
Collection ISSN: 2326-2699 (electronic)

Cover image licensed by Ingram Image, StockPhotoSecrets.com
Cover and interior design by S4Carlisle Publishing Services Private Ltd., Chennai, India

Third edition: 2021

10 9 8 7 6 5 4 3 2 1

Dedication

To family and friends—the value co-creators in my life.

Abstract

The service process design landscape is changing, with many of the previous limitations disappearing on how and by whom services are delivered. Opportunities for new service design configurations are being supported, to a large extent, by technology-enabled innovations; many tasks previously performed by the service provider may now be performed by either the customer or the service provider. As a result, customers are playing a more active role in the service process, not only through self-service but also by providing information to the service provider to create a more personalized service experience. *Designing Service Processes to Unlock Value* explores how service processes can be designed to leverage the expanding range of opportunities for service providers and customers to co-create value. Readers will learn about frameworks for value co-creation and models for designing all types of service processes, as well as the unique challenges of designing knowledge-intensive services. With the growing number of alternatives for designing service processes and determining who performs the various service tasks, service performance outcomes are increasingly dependent on the knowledge, skills, and abilities—that is, capabilities—of *both* service providers and customers. Thus, this book concludes with approaches to unlock these capabilities and further boost value co-creation.

The third edition of *Designing Service Processes to Unlock Value* was written in the midst of the COVID-19 global pandemic. This pandemic is having and will continue to have profound impacts on how services are designed, delivered, and experienced by service providers and customers, as well as the communities and world in which they live. I have included a number of examples of how services have been adapted or changed during the pandemic, some of which will likely translate to permanent shifts in the service process design landscape. In fact, process design options for all services are proliferating due to the explosive growth of evolving technologies such as robots, extended reality, artificial intelligence, Internet of Things, and other smart technologies. This edition includes new and updated examples of technology-enabled innovations that provide unprecedented flexibility in service process design and continue to transform how service providers and customers co-produce services. At the same time, readers will see how these and other service innovations can have important—and sometimes surprising—impacts on the nature of the benefit and cost trade-offs and synergies that determine value co-creation.

Keywords

customer; innovation; processes; self-service; services; service inventory; service process design; service provider; technology; value co-creation

Contents

Acknowledgments

No project is ever truly a solo effort, and I would like to thank everyone who has helped and encouraged me along the way.

First, thanks to Scott Isenberg from Business Expert Press, who suggested I write a book on a topic I am passionate about, which is how I came to write *Designing Service Processes to Unlock Value*. Scott fielded my many questions and assuaged my concerns during the process.

My colleagues Linda Boardman Liu and Mark Davis and my husband Richard Field read the book from cover to cover and provided constructive feedback and ideas for improvement. They were enthusiastic supporters of this project, for which I am extremely grateful.

I also want to acknowledge the role my students played in the writing of this third edition. The ideas and types of examples they found most interesting are the ones I have emphasized and expanded in this edition.

And finally, to my family—husband Richard and sons Ben, Evan, and Jon—all my love and gratitude for everything you have brought to my life.

Joy Field
June 2020

CHAPTER 1

Introduction

As firms strive to grow their revenues and profits, they increasingly look to services as a source of competitive advantage. Traditional service process designs—where the service provider takes the lead and the customer is the recipient of the service product—have given way to a different paradigm in which the service provider and customer work together to co-create value. Oftentimes this involves the use of innovative technologies that support new ways of delivering services. Service providers who embrace this model are enhancing their competitive position through service processes that provide more value to customers *and* higher profits to the firm.

But what exactly are service providers and customers doing to unlock the tremendous value co-creation potential from this new approach to service process design? Based on my research and experience, I wrote this book to help answer that question and to share the stories of how service firms and their customers are leveraging the new opportunities to design state-of-the-art service processes while confronting the inevitable challenges that arise.

Before continuing, it is important to be clear about what is meant by a *service process. Processes*, in general, can be defined as "any transformation that converts inputs to outputs."[1] Of course, for business processes, the goal is not just to convert inputs to outputs but to add value in the process. The elements of the transformation include a network of activities or tasks to be performed, along with the process resources (labor, capital, information) that are necessary to complete the tasks. For a *service* process, in particular, "the customer provides significant inputs [resources] into the production [transformation] process."[2] Customer

---

[1]Anupindi et al. (2012).
[2]Sampson and Froehle (2006).

inputs include self-inputs (themselves, their labor), tangible belongings (their property), and/or customer-provided information. In other words, customers and their resources are always involved in some way in their own service process.

An example of a supermarket grocery shopping process will help to make these concepts more concrete. For illustrative purposes, assume that the "transformation" process starts when customers arrive at the supermarket and ends when they complete their shopping. Inputs to the process include customers, their shopping lists, and payment method. The shopping process, in brief, involves finding the desired items, placing them in a cart (resource), and checking out. Other resources are the store itself, products on the shelves (or in the freezer, refrigerator, behind the counter), employees, information (e.g., signs indicating what types of products are in each aisle), and various technologies (e.g., for checkout). The outputs (or "service products") are the bagged and purchased groceries and (hopefully) satisfied customers.

But the in-store grocery shopping process is not immune to the changes happening in the increasingly dynamic business environment for services. In fact, the industry is undergoing the type of paradigm shift mentioned above. Traditional supermarkets are facing escalating competition due to the proliferation of store formats (convenience store to super-store) and from online delivery channels. Grocery services delivered through an online channel are now being offered by brick-and-mortar chains as well as online-only players such as Amazon Fresh and Peapod. More recently, online firms such as Blue Apron, Plated, and Hello Fresh have started delivering fresh ingredients to conveniently prepare meals at home, providing the exact amount of ingredients needed with no waste. In addition, changes to in-store processes are altering the way in which the service providers and customers co-create value; the introduction of new technologies—customer-operated scanners, self-service checkout, digital kiosks—allow (or, in some cases, require) customers to perform tasks previously done by store employees. However, the ever-evolving example of the self-service checkout should serve as a cautionary tale of the challenges firms encounter when changing the way services are delivered. In fact, a good starting point for identifying the opportunities and challenges facing service process designers is with self-service technologies and their incorporation into the service process.

Why Customers Love Automatic Teller Machines… But Have a Love/Hate Relationship with Self-Service Checkout

Consider two service processes we're all familiar with: personal banking and supermarket checkout. For years, both processes have had a self-service option—automatic teller machines (ATMs) and self-service checkout kiosks—yet, historically, ATMs have been met with a much higher level of customer acceptance and use. Why is that?

To answer the question we need to look at how each of these self-service options creates value for the participants in the service process and how it compares to the full-service option. *Value* is created when "benefits (including access to resources and capabilities) are perceived to be greater than costs—which include money, time, and effort—associated with obtaining these benefits."[3] For a service process to be provided by the firm and used by the customer, both parties must individually realize value. However, the value the firm and customers acquire from the service process are not independent of each other. Because of this, and due to the significant inputs that customers have into the service process, it follows then that joint firm and customer value is necessarily *co-created* through the interactions of service providers with the customers themselves, their property, and/or their information. (Note that co-creation is different from *co-production*; co-production refers specifically to the labor contributed by participants in the service process to complete service tasks.) With this in mind, let's contrast value co-creation for self-service banking using an ATM with self-service checkout at the supermarket.

From the perspective of a bank or a supermarket, these self-service technologies reduce the number of employees needed by transferring service tasks to the customers. So the customer's unpaid labor replaces the paid labor of the bank teller and the supermarket cashier. This labor cost

---

[3]Davis, Spohrer, and Maglio (2011).

reduction benefit is offset by the costs to buy, install, support, and maintain the ATMs and self-service checkouts. Support and maintenance costs for ATMs include access to employees when customers have questions or problems, collection of deposits and restocking cash, and preventative maintenance or unscheduled repair of a malfunctioning ATM. Self-service checkout kiosks still require employee support, with one employee monitoring several kiosks to aid customers, prevent theft, and verify purchases with age restrictions. Although support and maintenance costs are somewhat variable by customer volume, the cost of buying and installing an ATM or self-service checkout kiosk is essentially fixed. As a result, the value of these technologies to the firm increases as customer utilization of the self-service option increases and fewer employees are needed.

Although the basic value calculations from the firm's standpoint are similar for ATMs and self-service checkouts, they differ radically from the customer's viewpoint. First, think about *what* banking services are offered by an ATM. ATMs are designed so that only standardized and simple transactions such as withdrawing cash or depositing checks can be completed by the customer through this self-service channel. As a result, the customer interface with the ATM is correspondingly standardized and simple, making it easy for the customer to learn and use. For other banking services such as error resolution or renting or accessing a safe deposit box, the customer must still interact with a bank employee either because of the complexity of the service or for security reasons. Because the standard and simple services available from ATMs are also the most common ones, customers have the choice of using the ATM rather than a teller for a majority of their banking needs.

However, service task types are not as neatly separable when using self-service checkouts. While scanning barcodes on prepackaged products is straightforward, the checkout process for items without barcodes, such as fresh fruits and vegetables and bakery goods, is more complicated and involves entering the item identifier and the number of items. In fact, a study of checkout times at a discount retailer has found that for a similar basket of items, it takes an average of 50 percent longer for self-service checkout compared to full-service checkout with cashiers who are trained to efficiently handle all types of items. And to add to their burden, self-service customers are often responsible for performing additional steps not part of the full-service process—such as weighing the individual items—that help prevent theft. This is the situation faced by a typical customer with a mix of items when deciding whether to use self-service or full-service checkout. Compared with ATMs that limit self-service transactions to ones that are standardized and simple for the customer to perform, self-service checkout involves a wider range of task difficulty requiring more customer time and effort, which many customers, frankly, find intimidating.

But what about the benefits to customers? How do ATMs compare with self-service checkout? The most obvious benefit of ATMs is their convenience in terms of time and place; customers can access ATMs 24/7 at branches as well as other locations close to work and home. In fact, as the network of ATMs grows and accessing an ATM becomes even more convenient, the value of this self-service channel to the customer increases in what is known as a network effect. Customers are no longer limited to "banker's hours" for common transactions. In contrast, self-service checkout is available only during supermarket store hours and only for customers shopping at that particular store. In addition, three-quarters of the respondents to a Harris poll for Digimarc said that they sometimes avoid self-service checkouts often because of anticipated technical problems.[4] Another survey found that one in three shoppers have actually walked out of a store without the items they intended to buy because of a bad experience with a self-service checkout.[5]

Ironically, because many customers do not perceive that the benefits outweigh the costs, customers who *are* comfortable using self-service checkout may benefit if it results in underutilization of this channel.[6] And even customers who would otherwise be willing to use self-service checkout with a short line over full-service checkout with a longer line might think twice before choosing self-service. After all, any customer ahead of them in the self-service line is an unknown variable compared to the more reliable checkout process with a cashier.[7] Underutilization, in turn,

---

[4]Digimarc (2015).
[5]Tensator Group (2013).
[6]Curtis (2019).
[7]Postrel (2015).

negatively impacts the value of self-service checkout to the company as the expected employee labor reductions to offset the costs of the technology fail to materialize. To make matters worse, any negative experiences with other customers in self-service checkout lines spill over to perceptions of poor service quality provided by the supermarket—even if no supermarket employee was involved in the process.[8] The high perceived value of ATMs by customers, in contrast, contributes to the co-creation of value with the bank through high utilization, lower labor costs, and an expanded network of ATMs.

However, years of experience with self-service checkout has led to a better understanding of how customers perceive and use the technology. As a result, improvements in both the technology and in-store self-service checkout process have attempted to change the value equation for the customer by making self-service checkout more attractive. Newer self-service checkout screen designs have decreased the time to page through produce codes by highlighting the top-selling fruits and vegetables first or, if the customer scans a loyalty card, their own previous purchasing history.[9] Other innovations include moving this time-consuming and complicated part of the checkout process offline by providing scales with barcode printers next to the fresh fruits and vegetables. Sam's Club has taken the self-service concept further through the Scan & Go feature on their smartphone app that allows customers to scan and bag their items while they shop and quickly check out using the app.[10] Tesco has even redesigned its self-service checkouts to replace the "irritating and bossy" voice with a friendlier one and eliminated the phrase "unexpected item in the bagging area" that customers find annoying.[11] Other innovations include scanners that directly identify the item by shape and size, thus, relieving the customer of the task of choosing the correct code.[12] Interestingly, despite these changes to make the self-service checkout experience better, the divide between customers who like self-service and those who dislike it has actually intensified over time. On one hand, many

---

[8]Li et al. (2013).
[9]Postrel (2015).
[10]Sam's Club (2020).
[11]Hamacher (2017).
[12]Ibid.

customers—especially those in the 18- to 34-year-old demographic—actually prefer self-service; they like the convenience and control of do-it-yourself checkout and packing their own bags the way they want and prefer to interact with technology over humans.[13] Although a mistake can still abort the whole process, millennials, in particular, are comfortable dealing with technology glitches and figuring out how to solve them.[14] On the other hand, older demographics will overwhelmingly choose a cashier if both a self-service kiosk and cashier are available.[15] Many resent having to do the checkout work and are concerned over job losses with self-service. For the provider, theft remains a serious problem. In fact, self-service checkout theft has become so ubiquitous that a lingo has sprung up around it. For example, ringing up an expensive product using the code for a cheaper product is referred to as the "banana trick," with many customers justifying theft because of the extra work they do.[16]

As evidence that self-service checkout has evolved to better meet the needs of both customers and providers—including new technologies to detect theft—in 2019, large chains such as Costco, Big Y, and Albertson's began reintroducing or ramping up the use of self-service checkout kiosks after removing some or all of their kiosks earlier in the decade.[17] In 2013, Craig Jelinek, Costco CEO, stated that Costco was eliminating self-service checkout because "employees do a better job."[18] At the time, Jelinek and these other firms' executives arguably saw more value co-creation from the full-service checkout process than by enhancements to the self-service checkout technology. However, just a few years later, Richard Galanti, Costco EVP and CFO, had this to say about self-service checkout: "It's very fast and customers are using it … And it's saving some labor at the front end. As important, on the highest volume units, it's getting people through the front end faster."[19]

---

[13]Harris (2019).

[14]Dwyer (2019).

[15]Harris (2019).

[16]Chun (2018).

[17]Ryan (2019); Kinney (2019); Redman (2019); and Nassauer (2020).

[18]Lutz (2013).

[19]Ryan (2019).

As the examples of personal banking and supermarket checkout clearly show, service process design choices have a significant impact on how—and to what extent—value is co-created by the service provider and customer. Focusing on the self-service options for each of these services highlights how technology-enabled service innovations are altering the service process design landscape by allowing customers to perform what were previously service provider tasks. However, as the case of the supermarket self-service checkout illustrates, the road toward more self-service can be bumpy and the overall value equation is still being worked out. In fact, even in 2020, the *Wall Street Journal* asserts: "Stores and Shoppers Agree: Self-Checkout is Hard."[20] Given the much more complex process for supermarket self-service checkout than ATMs, it is unlikely that the former will ever be as frictionless as the latter. But ongoing advancements in the self-service checkout kiosk technology and processes will continue to increase the net value to stakeholders over time. And with more and more customers using self-service checkout to avoid contact with cashiers during the COVID-19 pandemic,[21] this may impact the long-term value equation by accelerating both customer acceptance of, and the rate of improvement in, the kiosk technology.

A Roadmap for the Book

By the end of this book, readers should understand how firms can gain a competitive advantage by designing service processes to make the most of the extraordinary opportunities available for value co-creation. Our journey begins by examining the changing nature of service processes in Chapter 2. Three trends—the rapid pace of technology-enabled service innovation, the expanded role of the customer, and the increasing use of service inventory—are largely responsible for the explosion of service process design options that are enabling service providers and customers to integrate their resources to co-create value in ways previously unimaginable.

---

[20]Nassauer (2020).
[21]Carlisle (2020).

We then delve further into the concept of value and what it means to each of the participants in the service process. The value co-creation framework in Figure 3.1 shows how the service process design brings these participants together to co-create value. The value co-creation measurement model then identifies the benefits, costs, trade-offs, and synergies to consider when assessing value co-creation. Chapter 3 concludes with a step-by-step process for designing service processes—including the trends from Chapter 2—to unlock value co-creation.

Next in Chapter 4, we focus on knowledge-intensive services such as managerial and technology consulting, health care, legal services, and education, in which the service process activities and service products are primarily centered on information and information flows. These complex and highly customized services are singled out because they present a few unique challenges for service process designers: although both the service provider and customer possess information necessary for the co-production of the knowledge-based service product, information transfers between the parties are often difficult and costly (i.e., "sticky"). In addition, as the actual service need is not always apparent at the start of the process, knowledge-intensive service contracts are often left incomplete and subject to renegotiation in real time. With these challenges in mind, Box 4.2 provides guidance for designing knowledge-intensive service processes that complement the design recommendations in Chapter 3.

Finally, the roadmap leads to the foundation of value co-creation—the capabilities of the service participants. In other words, unlocking value co-creation hinges on unlocking the capabilities of the service providers and customers. This occurs by integrating service provider and customer resources—themselves, information, equipment, materials—to improve the knowledge, skills, and abilities of each party. In Chapter 5, we see how service providers are unlocking the capabilities of customers; customers are unlocking the capabilities of service providers; and, most importantly, how the parties jointly unlock capabilities with a self-reinforcing cycle of "capability synergies." This book concludes with a series of questions that help service process designers determine which capabilities to unlock and how.

I hope you find our journey through this book to be one of value co-creation!

CHAPTER 2

The Changing Nature of Service Processes

In this chapter, we will look at three trends that have been instrumental in driving changes to the service process design landscape: the rapid pace of technology-enabled service innovation, the expanded role of the customer, and the increasing use of service inventory. Although each of these trends and their impact on service processes can be considered separately, in many cases, they are linked together through supporting technologies. Clearly, the expanded role of the customer has been facilitated by self-service technologies (SSTs). In addition, performing and storing a portion of the service work before the customer enters the service system (i.e., service inventory) is becoming increasingly common with information-based services. For example, an online platform, such as Google Finance (technology-enabled service innovation), contains stored information on financial products (service inventory) from which customers can construct and track their own portfolios (expanded role of the customer through self-service). In the next chapter, we will consider the implications of this changing landscape for service process design and value co-creation.

Technology-Enabled Service Innovation

Bank automatic teller machines (ATMs) and supermarket self-service checkout kiosks are just two examples of technology-enabled service innovations that have revolutionized not only how services are delivered but also how customers experience services. Ideally, these technologies result in "faster, better, and cheaper"—that is, higher value—services from the perspectives of both the customer and the service provider, objectives that have been largely met in the case of ATMs.

All of us are familiar with these and other SSTs because we frequently interact with them as part of the service process. But SSTs are only the tip of the iceberg. Other technologies are being deployed throughout the service supply chain that are opaque to the customer but undeniably contribute to value creation.

Figure 2.1 depicts the service supply chain, with the arrows representing physical and information flows among its members and with the external environment. Innovative technologies are being used to support or automate these flows, as well as the process activities for the service provider, customers, and suppliers. Likewise, these technologies are enabling new service delivery models where customers interact not only with their direct service provider but also with other service suppliers in the system (e.g., through platforms for peer-to-peer services, as discussed later in this section).

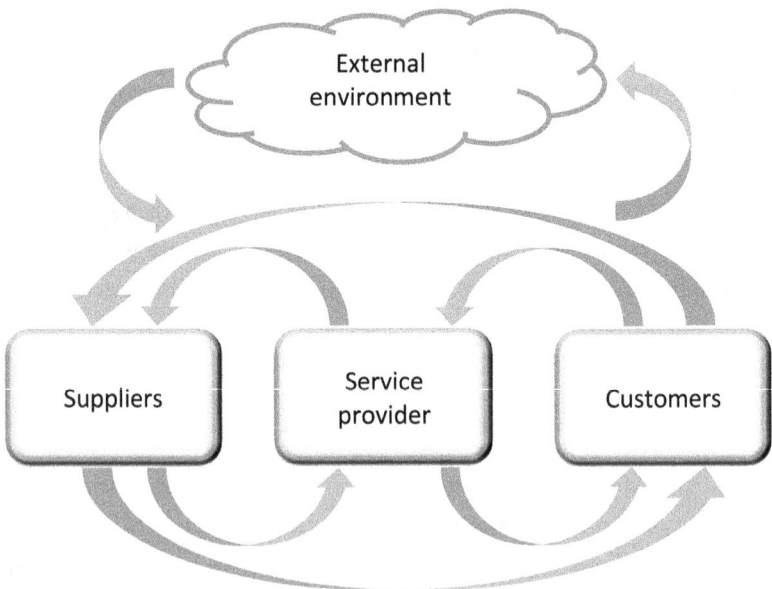

Figure 2.1 Service supply chain

We will return later to the question of how service process design choices—including the use of technology—drive value. But, first, let's take a look at some of the types of technology-enabled service innovations that have been applied throughout the service supply chain.

Self-Service Technologies

Service providers today are asking customers to perform more of the service process tasks and are providing SSTs to help them to do their part. These technologies are also facilitating physical and information flows between service participants. Take the ubiquitous self-service gas pump, for example. Following the step-by-step instructions displayed on the unit, customers insert a credit card to start the service, pump gas, and collect a receipt at the end. This service process involves the customer performing a service task (pumping gas), information flow from the service provider to the customer (instructions), information flow from the customer to the service provider (credit card information), and physical flow from the service provider to the customer (gas).

Although pumping one's own gas often reduces the wait for the gas station attendant—usually the bottleneck resource—some providers have moved back to a full-service model. Interestingly, the pervasiveness of the self-service channel, and the resulting relative scarcity of the full-service channel, has highlighted the distinct value proposition of *each* service process channel for different customer segments, or for varying customer preferences within a segment (such as full-service on rainy days for customers who usually use self-service).

SSTs for Customer Transactions and Customer Service

From ATMs to self-service checkout kiosks to self-service gas pumps, technologies geared toward self-service customer transactions are all around us. The explosion of self-service processes is due, to a large extent, to online services and e-commerce, in particular. Virtually an unlimited range of transactions can be done online through a computer or mobile device—buying, selling, banking, bill pay, and so on. In addition to the basic transactional functionality of e-commerce websites, process features for storing customer information, enabling customer search, and using provider recommendation engines to supplement or replace customer search have other benefits: faster online checkout, lower customer search costs, *and* increased sales.[1]

New technologies, such as augmented reality, are also helping consumers decide which transactions to make in the first place. Lowe's, a retailer specializing in home improvement, recently introduced "View in Your Space," an augmented reality feature on their app, that allows customers to scan their surroundings and drag and drop Lowe's products into a customer's space to see how they fit in.[2] This feature helps address the visualization barriers that contribute to the abandonment of billions of dollars in home improvement projects each year. Similarly, Macy's app allows customers to use augmented reality to virtually "try on" various beauty products prior to purchase.[3]

Even "customer service" has become, to a large degree, "customer self-service" both online (e.g., package tracking and frequently asked questions [FAQs]) and by phone using interactive voice response systems (IVRs). Much has been written about customer frustration with IVRs, especially difficulty in reaching a live customer service representative. In fact, a number of IVR "cheat sheets" can be found online (e.g., GetHuman.com) that inform consumers which keys to push to circumvent the automated system and speak with a real person.[4] Although firms like Zappos, an online retailer of shoes, consider customer service to be a core competency and have always focused on building their call center operations around human interaction, a number of other firms have been rethinking and redesigning their call center operations to reestablish the person-to-person connection. For example, Citi's "Simplicity" credit card advertisements from a few years ago acknowledged customer frustration with IVRs and encouraged

---

[1]De, Hu, and Rahman (2010).
[2]Lowes (2018).
[3]Macy's (2019).
[4]GetHuman (2020).

customers to "just press zero anytime" to speak with a customer representative. Many firms are even more proactive with online customer service by monitoring individual customer activity on their website to infer when the customer is searching for the answer to a question or has another customer service need and displaying a pop-up window asking if the customer would like to "chat" with an employee. While online customer service and IVRs consistently deliver on the promise of lower costs and increased customer convenience for simple transactional tasks (e.g., obtaining a flight status), the IVR value proposition is less straightforward for more complex services where interactions with employees are often necessary.

SSTs for Education and Health Care

The use of SSTs for educational and healthcare purposes is growing by leaps and bounds. Online and distance learning and training (e-learning) is now available for virtually any type of organizational and educational need. One popular platform for e-learning is Blackboard, a learning management system for K-12, higher education, continuing education, corporate, government, and military markets.[5] The Blackboard platform is versatile: it can be used in both synchronous (real time) and asynchronous (self-directed) learning modes; and its functionalities include access to course content and training modules, discussion boards, virtual collaborative spaces, mobile learning resources (i.e., students can interact with the instructor, other students, and Blackboard through their mobile devices), multiple modes of instructor–student communication, social network capabilities—to name just a few. Blackboard also has analytics functionality to optimize both institutional and student outcomes. One of its analytics tools, Blackboard Predict, identifies at-risk students to help instructors increase course completion and student retention rates.

During the COVID-19 pandemic, in-person classroom instruction moved to online and distance learning. A Blackboard infographic

---

[5]Blackboard (2020).

on the impact of COVID-19 on education attests to the scale and scope of this transition. For example, Blackboard Collaborate, the platform's virtual learning solution, saw a whopping 3,600 percent increase in global daily users during March 2020.[6] Other instructors are accessing tools outside their learning management systems for their virtual classrooms. One popular tool for videoconferencing and recording classes is Zoom, which has seen the maximum number of daily users increase from 10 million per day as of the end of December 2019 to 200 million per day in March 2020.[7] However, the rapid increase in users highlighted some technical weaknesses and vulnerabilities that Zoom quickly attempted to address. One such vulnerability, "Zoombombing," a term popularized during the COVID-19 pandemic, refers to "the unwanted intrusion into a video conference call by an individual, which causes disruption."[8] Despite these and other glitches, many question whether the adjustments made during the pandemic may portend a more permanent shift toward online and distance learning.[9]

In the area of healthcare education, Pursuant Health,[10] a healthcare technology and data analytics firm, has installed over 4,600 kiosks in high-traffic retail pharmacy settings to provide access to self-service healthcare screening and education tools, including consumers who might not otherwise have convenient access to health care. Their kiosks offer vision, blood pressure, and body mass index testing. In addition, they connect users with local providers and provide a basic health risk assessment and free online account with a personalized dashboard to track health changes—empowering consumers to take a more hands-on role in their own health care. With advances in self-service kiosk technology, we will continue to see more use cases in the healthcare industry (Box 2.1).

---

[6]Blackboard infographic (2020).

[7]Zoom blog (2020).

[8]Wikipedia, Zoombombing (2020).

[9]Marcus (2020).

[10]Pursuant Health (2020).

Box 2.1

Self-service check-in kiosks at your health care provider

An increasing number of healthcare systems, including hospitals, clinics, and medical practices, are installing patient check-in kiosks as an alternative to checking in with staff at the front desk. As with airport kiosks, patients simply press a touchscreen and follow the step-by-step instructions to check in and securely access and update their personal records. Patients are finding that learning to use the kiosks results in benefits such as shorter waits and a standardized and predictable check-in process. These benefits add up, especially for patients with chronic conditions and others who frequently visit their healthcare providers. For the healthcare provider, the check-in process is more efficient, which means fewer staff are needed—and the remaining staff are now available to focus on more complex services. One large hospital organization initially projected that 25 percent of their patients would use the kiosks, well below the actual 60 percent usage rate. Moreover, they saw an 80 percent reduction in form costs, 84 percent reduction in check-in costs, and a 65 percent increase in patient co-payment collections—along with a significant increase in patient satisfaction scores. Using a kiosk also addresses Health Insurance Portability and Accountability Act (HIPAA) concerns because the gathering of patient-specific information during check-in (e.g., the patient's medical condition and financial matters) is no longer verbalized. The kiosks produced by Connected Technology Solutions (CTS)[11] are HIPAA compliant; they offer privacy options as per HIPAA guidelines and require the user to be directly in front of the screen to read the display, preventing others from seeing personal information. Their adjustable floor standing models with audio also meet the Americans with Disabilities Act standards. With a 40-inch range of vertical motion, the kiosks are as accessible to patients in wheelchairs as to someone standing, enabling all patients to use this check-in method. As of 2020, over 250 million patient check-ins have been processed through CTS kiosks.

---

[11]This box is based on information from Connected Technology Solutions (2020) and a presentation by Sandra Nix, CTS CEO, at Customer Engagement Technology World in San Francisco on April 27, 2011.

New applications of SSTs in health care are also enabling greater patient participation in their diagnosis and treatment processes. Recent innovations include Eve Medical's home Pap smear kits to detect cervical cancer, Quanovate's self-service tool that tracks women's fertility using artificial intelligence (AI), and Sword Health's physiotherapy at home using a Bluetooth-connected motion sensor tracker coupled with a virtual physical therapist.[12] In the area of disease management, Teva Pharmaceutical's ProAir Digihaler, a digital inhaler with built-in sensors, helps patients with asthma and chronic obstructive pulmonary disease (COPD) to better manage their conditions.[13] The sensors detect use of the inhaler and measure inspiratory flow, with the data sent to a companion mobile app using Bluetooth technology. This allows patients to review the information on inhaler usage and efficacy, and, if desired, share it with a healthcare provider—both increasing patient engagement in their care and improving outcomes. These technologies are tapping into the growing demand for home testing and disease management SSTs, supported by evidence that self-service can produce high-quality outcomes. For example, a 2018 study found that the lab results were comparable for women using home HPV kits and those who were tested in person.[14]

The examples in this section are, admittedly, a small sampling of the wide variety and functions of SSTs. Although the specifics vary, each of these—as well as the many other SSTs—shapes the design of the customer tasks and information and physical flows between the customer, service provider, and their suppliers. While SSTs have been a great value creation engine in general, an unanticipated outcome of their widespread use has been to call attention to the benefits of full service—as gas station operators have discovered. Evaluating the pros and cons of self-service and full-service channels can help the firm meet the needs of different customer segments by clarifying how and under what conditions each channel creates value, as well as by identifying opportunities to better design the underlying service processes.

---

[12]Stone (2019).

[13]Teva Pharmaceutical (2020).

[14]Des Marais et al. (2018).

Technologies for Service Providers

At the hub of the service supply chain, the service provider performs service process tasks and interfaces with customers, suppliers, and the external environment. In fact, within the service supply chain, the service provider has a dual role—not only as a supplier to its customers but also as a customer to its suppliers. As with SSTs and customers, technologies that focus on the service provider have impacted how their tasks and interactions with other supply chain members are carried out. Let's look at some examples.

Customer-Facing Tasks

Call centers have been at the forefront of technology innovation adoption, not only to enable self-service with IVRs but also to support the frontline employees in their interactions with customers. Call center management software, either purchased or developed internally, can be used to link information that customers key into their phone to their customer accounts when they contact the call center. This information is then automatically pulled up as calls are routed to customer service representatives. The software is designed to eliminate the need for customers to provide the same information more than once and streamlines the process to reduce "talk time," typically a key call center performance indicator. Firms are also applying technology solutions to link all customer service touchpoints—phone, online chat, email, social media, in-person—to further improve process efficiency and ensure that customers have a consistent experience across customer service channels.

In general, detailed customer databases acquired through customer interactions support customer relationship management (CRM) efforts and the personalization of services. In a survey of in-home services (cable or satellite television, Internet, utilities, retail home deliveries, or other mobile workforce-related services) conducted by the Economist Intelligence Unit,[15] respondents identified "tracking customer preferences and previous requirements" as the most important service delivery practice for improving an in-home service firm's competitive position. In fact, a wide range of customer tracking software products is available to meet the

---

[15]Waldie (2011).

needs of large companies down to small businesses. Modern Pest Services, a family-owned pest control company in New England, has introduced a smaller-scale version of a tracking system that allows customer information to be captured, consolidated, and available to contact employees—with similar benefits to those achieved by much larger companies. AI and predictive analytic capabilities embedded in tracking and CRM software (e.g., Salesforce) amplify these benefits through data-driven recommendations for more personalized and proactive services to meet current and anticipated future customer needs.

Technology innovations are also having a significant impact on healthcare delivery processes. Telemedicine, in which healthcare providers care for patients remotely, has seen its popularity spike during the COVID-19 pandemic. However, a barrier to widespread adoption of telemedicine is that the technologies used must be in compliance with the Health Insurance Portability and Accountability Act (HIPAA), which protects the privacy of personal health information. Companies have responded by developing HIPAA compliant videoconferencing tools. For example, the product offered by VSee has military-grade encryption and functionality to meet the particular needs of this market, including secure video chat and screen share and live annotation to simulate an in-person meeting.[16]

In the surgical suite, many procedures that once required a large incision and a long recovery time can now be done using a laparoscopic or minimally invasive approach with small incisions and a shorter recovery. The laparoscopes used in these procedures are fitted with a camera and light to provide a view of the operative field while surgeons manipulate specially designed instruments that fit through the incisions. Further advances in robotics and communication technologies have even ushered in the early stages of remote surgery where the surgeon and patient are physically separated.

Other technologies are being applied to tasks that support the core surgical activities. Retained surgical items (RSIs), which include sponges, needles, clamps, or any other surgical items accidentally left in the patient's body after surgery, are considered a "never event"—a medical error that should never occur. Yet the manual system of counting sponges is

---

[16]VSee (2020).

prone to error in the complex and hectic operating room environment. To ideally eliminate retained sponges, a team at the Mayo Clinic Rochester introduced a data-matrix-coded sponge (DMS) system.[17] Each sponge and towel in the surgical suite has a unique data-matrix tag, otherwise known as a quick response or QR code. Before the item is used, it is scanned into the case ledger using a data-matrix scanner. At the conclusion of the procedure and after all sponges have been scanned out, the scanner confirms that the sponge count is correct. An incorrect sponge count triggers a search for the missing item(s), and the case cannot be closed out until all sponges originally scanned in have been accounted for. Prior to the implementation of the DMS system, the average interval between retained sponges was 64 days. For the 3-year tracking period following implementation, the Mayo Clinic Rochester reported zero sponge RSIs.

Back Office Support

In the banking, credit card, insurance, and other industries, fraud detection software is supporting the efforts of service providers to prevent—or at least quickly identify—potentially fraudulent transactions or claims. The software automates the process of detecting unusual activity and other predictors of fraud. Credit card companies, for example, with large customer bases could not realistically manually monitor all credit card activity in real time. Instead, they respond to alerts triggered by the software's fraud detection models and contact the credit card holder or place a temporary hold on the account pending a determination of actual fraudulent activity. The financial effects of these efforts are substantial; Markerstudy, an insurance company based in the United Kingdom, uses big data and visualization tools, such as Zoomdata, to save millions annually as a result of better fraud detection.[18]

Technologies under the umbrella of electronic data interchange (EDI) are used to manage information flows throughout the service supply chain, mainly for back office processes in both manufacturing and service firms. Although EDI systems have been in use for years, a more recent

---

[17]Cima et al. (2011).
[18]Mehta (2019).

application is "touchless" sales order and invoice processing. Products such as Conexiom eliminate paper sales orders and invoices and manual entry, increase data accuracy, and seamlessly integrate with customer and supplier systems.[19] Both Conexiom and Workday, a software vendor for back office functions such as payroll, have moved back office support to a cloud-based software model.[20] Workday's customers, for example, do not install or maintain the software themselves. Rather, the work gets done in Workday's own data centers and users simply pull the results in over the Internet. This saves the customer time and money (the cost is half of traditional systems) for what is normally a noncore activity, while benefiting from Workday's expertise and continuing technical innovation.

A new back office support technology, collaborative robots or "cobots," can be found in physically demanding environments such as warehouse order fulfillment. Unlike standard robots, cobots are designed to work with employees and "employ visual sensors and rely on sensitivity to physical contact and lower operational velocities to ensure workers can operate safely in close proximity to them."[21] Although cobots are still a small part of the global robot market, advances in machine-learning techniques coupled with cost reductions in technology are broadening the scope of potential applications. Current service applications include 6 River Systems' "Chuck," a warehouse cobot that intelligently groups orders and leads product pickers through work zones to minimize walking and increase productivity. Chuck carries the totes, allowing associates to pick hands-free, and delivers the products to takeoff locations for shipping. Office Depot replaced their previous cart pick process, which required associates to push and pull heavy carts, with Chucks. As a result, associated back, shoulder, wrist, and other injuries have gone to zero, while at the same time productivity and order accuracy have risen.[22] Technology innovation has impacted not only routine service provider tasks but also knowledge-intensive tasks. Moreover, new technologies are increasingly pushing the boundaries with solutions for tasks previously considered too difficult to automate (Box 2.2).

---

[19]Conexiom (2020).
[20]Lyons (2012).
[21]Halder (2019).
[22]6 River Systems (2020).

Box 2.2

Software support for text and speech analytics

The discovery phase of a lawsuit, in which each party obtains and scrutinizes evidence from the opposing party, frequently generates a tremendous amount of paper documents and digital materials, all of which must be searchable by the legal team. Firms such as Xact Data Discovery[23] provide document scanning services to digitize the paper documents and index the materials in a searchable format. But Xact's main business line is the search process itself. At the direction of their law firm client who provides a list of keywords and other search specifications, Xact performs the search and delivers the results to the client in an agreed-upon format. For large cases, Xact's dedicated resources and scalability allow for a faster turnaround, which is critical with court-imposed deadlines. As one client noted, law firms' search needs are often idiosyncratic to the case, especially for large and complex cases, and rely on the tacit knowledge of the legal team to structure the search and make sense of the results. As a result, developing a close working relationship with Xact is critical to fostering the joint understanding of the client needs necessary for producing high-quality results efficiently. With the search results, legal professionals can now more quickly analyze evidence over the entire digital collection of discovery documents. Manpower needs, for what was previously an extremely labor-intensive process, are significantly reduced.

In addition, the technologies for speech analytics are becoming increasing sophisticated, with software that not only captures the content but also subjective characteristics of speech. Call center employees have long been evaluated on metrics such as average call length, first call resolution, and information accuracy, with much of this data collected through automated processes. Until recently, rating and coaching agents on more subjective measures, which capture the quality of the agent/customer interaction and other aspects of the

---

[23]This box is based on information from the Xact Data Discovery website (accessed April 12, 2020): www.xactdatadiscovery.com and an interview with a law firm client.

customer experience, has remained a manual process, requiring managers or quality assurance to listen in on a sample of calls. But now, even these processes are being automated. Cogito, a market leader in this space, combines artificial intelligence and machine learning with insights from behavioral research to perform in-call voice analysis on both agents and customers.[24] Its algorithms assess subjective agent attributes such as energy, professionalism, empathy, tone, and pace, as well as customer emotional responses such as frustration. Based on its analysis of the interaction, Cogito provides real-time guidance through alerts such as "Speaking Quickly" or "Empathy Cue" to trigger adjustments in agent speaking behaviors to improve the customer experience. Real-time dashboards enable managers to monitor and intervene in live calls, while call center analytics help identify actionable best practices and trends. But not everyone is convinced that Cogito is enhancing employee performance—and some think that the system can be gamed. Anecdotes from agents include empathy alerts triggered by any tonal variation, including laughter, and saying "sorry" frequently—even if unwarranted—just to meet empathy metrics.[25] So it seems that for the time being, at least, speech analytics for understanding and responding to emotions may still require something of a human touch.

Employee Hiring

The supplier technologies discussed so far in this section have focused on operational tasks and interactions with supply chain partners. However, even traditionally low-tech processes such as employee hiring are becoming more technology-based. In fact, the hiring process is undergoing a sea change with the use of artificial intelligence to screen resumes and evaluate the performance of candidates during interviews.

---

[24]Cogito (2020).
[25]Dzieza (2020).

As the volume of online applications continues to grow, many firms have moved to using AI and machine-learning systems to save time and money, as well as to potentially reduce the biases humans bring to the resume vetting process.[26] These systems scan for specific keywords—both hard and soft skills—in the resume, and often have additional functionality to gauge applicants, such as knockout questions to eliminate unsuitable applicants early in the hiring process (e.g., ability to perform key job functions) and skills testing. Although this takes humans out of the initial screening process, the algorithms used are typically "trained" using data from the current workforce, which can introduce its own set of biases. If the workforce composition lacks diversity, these dominant attributes (e.g., gender, age, race) can be perpetuated unintentionally in the hiring recommendations.[27] For example, an AI-based system trained on data from a mostly male workforce may downgrade applications listing sports typically played by females, such as field hockey. Taken to an absurd extreme, "one vendor built a resume-screening tool that tagged being named Jared and playing high school lacrosse as predictors of success."[28] To better align a resume with the algorithms, job search professionals recommend using keywords and phrases from the job description and clear job titles that show increasing responsibility and impact.

Technology is also playing a growing role in the next stage of the hiring process—the interview.[29] Hiring firms are utilizing video interviewing technologies, developed by companies such as HireVue, to more efficiently winnow down the candidate pool to a smaller group of promising prospects for in-person interviews. The technology works by recording a candidate's answers to predetermined questions delivered on camera through a computer or smartphone.[30] Hiring managers can review the footage themselves and/or have recorded answers evaluated by AI. HireVue's algorithms not only analyze word choice and grammar but also more subjective attributes such as body language, facial expressions, and

---

[26]Shellenbarger (2019).

[27]Pietenpol (2019).

[28]Shellenbarger (2019).

[29]Schellmann (2020).

[30]Metz (2020).

voice tonality and cadence. Candidates are compared to current employ-ees who answered the same questions on video and evaluated on how well they match these employees.[31] Some have questioned the validity of algorithms that predict job success based on these subjective attributes, but HireVue claims their assessments are based on "100 percent validated science."[32] While the algorithms are something of a black box, interview coaches recommend adjusting the camera to eye level to maintain eye contact with the "interviewer" and, as with resumes, using keywords and phrases from the job description.

With the proliferation of technologies for service providers—as well as those for customer self-service discussed earlier—the service process design landscape is indeed dynamic. We next discuss technologies that continue to push the envelope and let service participants engage and interact with the service supply chain in new and different ways.

Platform Technologies for Peer-to-Peer Services

An increasing number of services are moving from a traditional service delivery model to a peer-to-peer (P2P) model. Perhaps the best-known example of a P2P service is Uber (also referred to as a sharing economy or gig economy service). Uber, and similar P2P services such as Airbnb, create platforms using existing technologies, with "peers"—in the roles of both customer and service supplier—transacting directly through the platform. The platform technology not only facilitates peer self-service but also provides services such as payment processing and quality assur-ance (e.g., rating systems) to deliver a frictionless experience. The plat-form technology takes the place of a trusted middleman by, for example, ensuring that the peer customer receives the expected service and the peer service provider is paid.

Another industry with a huge online presence supported by platform providers is the dating industry. In fact, dating apps are now so main-stream that the terms "swipe right" and "swipe left"—popularized by the dating app Tinder—have entered common usage as slang for showing

---

[31]Burke (2019).
[32]Ibid.

approval or disapproval, respectively. As with other P2P platforms, the platform technology lets peers connect directly, increasingly using AI and machine learning to better match its customers with each other. During the COVID-19 pandemic, many of these dating apps added virtual dating services, including livestreaming and video chat as a "social distancing" dating option.[33] However, these new features have broader safety implications, especially for first dates, and may change the online dating process for good—even after the virus threat has passed. JWed, an online dating service for Jewish singles, is taking virtual dating services to the next level and "plans to roll out other features—to use before and after video dates—'to replicate in-person dating as best we can.'"[34]

Although these platforms connect peers directly with each other, platform providers still act as intermediaries that dictate terms and conditions and collect fees to either join the platform or for transactions. Several startups have attempted to upend this model using decentralized platforms based on blockchain technology.[35] For example, BeeToken and SnagRide introduced decentralized, blockchain-based platforms to compete with Airbnb and Uber, respectively.[36] Their platforms use "smart contracts" that automatically self-execute without the need for an intermediary when the terms of the contract are met. Rather than rely on a revenue model based on transaction fees, many of these startups intended to ride the rising value of tokens sold to investors through initial coin offerings (analogous to selling stock)—a financial model that proved to be unsustainable.[37] Although firms such as BeeToken have attempted to pivot to a more conventional platform revenue model, these decentralized platforms have yet to make meaningful inroads into the P2P industry.

---

[33]Muzaffar (2020).

[34]Ibid.

[35]Blockchain is a distributed ledger that verifies and records transactions in blocks through the consensus of the nodes in its network. This technology is considered to be especially secure for two key reasons. First, because each block is tied to the previous block in a chain, it is impossible to change one block without changing the entire blockchain. In addition, information about the blocks is distributed to all the nodes in the network, so making a change would require agreement among the nodes.

[36]Vilner (2018).

[37]Dale (2019).

Smart, Connected Technologies for Service Innovation

Most of the technologies described so far in this chapter require the active involvement of the customer, service provider, and/or their suppliers in the service process. However, some services are being delivered with little or no human intervention using technologies such as the Internet of Things (IoT)—a network of smart, connected devices or "things" that communicate and exchange information directly with each other.[38] These smart devices do not simply communicate; they also react to the information being exchanged and, by doing so, engage in a service process. Although IoT devices typically use sense and respond capabilities to perform services that require no human involvement (e.g., smart thermostats with sensors that detect room occupancy and respond by adjusting the temperature accordingly), some smart services are triggered more directly by customer actions.[39]

As an example of the latter type of smart service, customers expecting a human service provider during hotel check-in are increasingly finding themselves interacting, instead, with a social robot. Social robots are physical "conversational agents" with humanoid forms, in contrast to virtual assistants such as Siri and Alexa, which are disembodied conversational agents. The defining characteristics of all conversational agents are that they "accept natural language as input and generate natural language as output in order to engage in a social conversation with its users."[40] "Pepper," a social robot from SoftBank Robotics, uses AI to recognize faces and emotions, can understand and converse with customers in 15 languages, and has 20 degrees of freedom for natural and expressive movements.[41] As a result, Pepper is able to engage with customers and adapt to their needs in a more "human-like" way (even posing for selfies with customers!) More than 15,000 Pepper social robots are deployed worldwide to perform services such as hotel check-in, airport customer service, shopping assistance, and fast-food checkout.[42] Other physical

---

[38]Jolt Consulting Group (2015).
[39]Verhoef et al. (2017).
[40]De Keyser et al. (2019).
[41]SoftBank Robotics (2020).
[42]Latham and Ling (2019).

robots have been invaluable during the COVID-19 pandemic. "Spot" is a robot that resembles a large dog and is being used outside hospitals to triage potential coronavirus patients.[43] It is fitted with an iPad that displays a doctor located in the hospital and has a camera and microphone to aid in diagnoses. Spots have also been retrofitted to deliver small items, such as water bottles, to patients to eliminate the need for caregivers to use scarce protective equipment for these service tasks.

Remote monitoring for inventory management is an IoT-enabled service in a retail setting. Sensors at the retailers convey inventory information to vendors, with automatic replenishment based on the inventory level at the retailer—or based on a more complex algorithm that takes into account a combination of data from other IoT devices including shipping times, production lags, and vendor inventory. Using a different solution to manage inventory, Target has adopted a "smart" RFID label program to improve inventory accuracy and enhance in-stock performance.[44] And remote monitoring of equipment at a customer site enables proactive (and often, remotely delivered) after-sales maintenance and repair services based on information from the equipment indicating a maintenance need or imminent failure[45] (see Box 2.4 for a detailed example of remote monitoring).

Health care too has seen the introduction of an ongoing stream of smart technology applications. Going back to the previous example of ProAir Digihaler for managing asthma and COPD, the data collected by the device belongs to the user for self-monitoring. But it can also be shared electronically with healthcare providers, adding another node in the service ecosystem. An even smaller healthcare IoT device is a sensor the size of a grain embedded in sensor-enabled pills.[46] When patients ingest these pills, the sensor sends a signal to a patch on the patient's body with the time the pill was taken, as well as other patient vitals. This information is relayed to healthcare providers who can monitor the patient and manage treatment. And inside an ambulance, an IoT-connected

---

[43]Bray (2020a).
[44]Swedberg (2015).
[45]Gandhi and Gervet (2016).
[46]Kuzela (2015).

defibrillator can feed data to the hospital so that it can put resources in place based on the patient's condition.[47] But to ward off health problems in the first place, virtual fitness coaches, using AI to offer personalized at-home training, are now an alternative to human personal trainers for meeting fitness goals.[48] The options range from free apps such as Freeletics, which offer AI-based training plans, to Tonal's home-based workout system that attaches to a wall. Tonal's AI personal trainer assesses the "client's" initial fitness level and changes the fitness routine as the client gets stronger.

Just as the AI algorithms powering virtual fitness coaches learn and improve with more data, Apple Maps learns about a user's travel preferences through data generated by their smartphone to predict where the user might want to go next—and then suggests a travel route. In general, tracking technologies for smartphones and other connected devices facilitate the delivery of services—whether or not the identity of the customer is known; for example, an individual's website click pattern can be tracked to learn a user's profile and offer real-time promotions and personalized service based only on the customer's usage behavior. We will come back to these and other similar examples later in the chapter as tools for creating service inventory and incorporating it in the service delivery process.

Smart technologies are not only changing how services are delivered to consumers and businesses but their applications extend to services with a broader impact on society. So-called "smart city" initiatives leverage the capabilities of smart technologies to improve the delivery of services to its citizens. More specifically, a smart city is "an urban area that uses different types of ... sensors to collect data and then uses insights gained from that data to manage assets, resources, and services efficiently."[49] For example, Alibaba's City Brain uses AI to analyze data from traffic light video feeds and GPS to improve traffic flow and reduce gridlock in Hangzhou, China.[50] Additionally, a number of major cities around the world have introduced "smart bins" to optimize trash collection. They

---

[47]Merrill (2019).

[48]Fosco (2019).

[49]Wikipedia, Smart city (2020).

[50]Hasija et al. (2020).

come equipped with compaction technology to increase effective bin capacity by 25 percent and sensors to alert trash collectors only when bins are 85 percent full to reduce collection trips. In a vital public health application, Kinsa Health created a "Health Weather Map," using data from hundreds of thousands of its smart thermometers across the U.S., to identify COVID-19 hotspots based on unusually high rates of fever.[51]

While the examples presented so far are already part of the existing service landscape, a provocative smart city idea from IBM Research labs is to use parked cars as a service delivery platform.[52] Recognizing that cars are parked over 95 percent of the time and their battery power, information processing and storage, and sensing capabilities are not being utilized while parked, researchers have proposed networking parked cars to create a service delivery platform. Possible applications are wide-ranging: cars parked at tourist attractions could create a WiFi backbone to store and share site maps and information with nearby tourists through their mobile phones. Using sensing capabilities, parked cars could be used to locate a wandering dementia patient wearing a Bluetooth bracelet or detect and locate gas leaks. As car manufacturers continue to improve the power and digital capabilities of their products, the range of possible service applications will continue to grow.

Interfacing with the External Environment

Although the focus of this book is primarily on the participants in the service supply chain shown in Figure 2.1, service activities also affect external stakeholders, including the communities and the world in which service firms operate. And external stakeholders are clamoring for increased transparency into how and to what extent they are impacted by these service activities. High on their wish list is more information on the environmental impacts of service firms, and a number of third-party organizations are stepping up with platforms to collect, aggregate, and disseminate this information. CDP (formerly the Carbon Disclosure Project) is an international nonprofit organization that runs the "global environmental

---

[51]Malloy (2020).
[52]Cooley (2014).

disclosure system." This system acts as one of the largest clearinghouses for investors, purchasers, and community stakeholders to access information on the carbon footprint, water usage, and other environmental metrics and associated risks for firms and their supply chain partners.[53] In 2019, over 120 major buyers, with a collective purchasing power of $3 trillion, asked their suppliers to disclose through CDP, with over 8,400 companies reporting requested environmental information. As a result, stakeholders can gain an end-to-end view of a firm's environmental impact. For example, a retailer's total carbon footprint—which includes not only its own operations but also those of its logistics providers and other suppliers—can be estimated using CDP platform analytics.

Service providers are also formalizing information flows with the external environment through "open innovation" processes. Rather than limiting service design activities to an internal development team, open innovation involves accessing ideas and innovations both outside the firm and from other employees inside the firm. With open innovation processes, firms establish a platform from which they can access potentially useful—but distributed—knowledge from nontraditional sources.[54] In most open innovation implementations, the Internet has been a facilitating technology that, in effect, expands direct participation in the service supply chain from these previously untapped sources. The Internet not only plays a key role in fostering awareness—for example, about innovation competitions—in the external environment but also functions as a means to manage the open innovation process.

One of the best-known examples of open innovation in services is the Netflix Prize, a competition sponsored by Netflix in 2006 for improving the accuracy of their existing movie recommendation system for predicting which movies their customers would like.[55] Netflix publicized the competition and invited any interested party to work on the project (also known as "crowdsourcing"), with a $1 million prize to the winner. From a field of over 40,000 teams from 186 countries, BellKor, a consortium of previously competing teams, emerged as the winner in 2009,

---

[53]CDP (2020).
[54]Byrum and Bingham (2015).
[55]This example is based on information from Idea Connection (2009).

with an improvement over Netflix's in-house recommendation system of more than 10 percent. This is an example of an "outside-in" approach, where a company makes greater use of external ideas and technologies in its own business.[56] Another version of open innovation is an "inside-out" approach, where a company allows some of its own ideas, technologies, or processes to be used by other businesses (e.g., Amazon partnering with other retailers to either or both develop and host their websites).

Although, in theory, ideas and innovations can flow into and out of the firm from and to anywhere in the external environment, it is often the service supply chain partners—suppliers and customers—who have the most to gain from engaging in the exchange of ideas and innovations. For example, IBM's "First-of-a-Kind" (FOAK) program was an innovation partnership with clients to develop and test new technologies that provide the client with a solution ahead of the competition and a potential commercialized product offering by IBM.[57] One successful project, developed in collaboration with a Danish hospital system, is a medical information hub for accessing electronic medical records that uses an "avatar" of the human body as a graphical interface for navigating a patient's file.[58] The user-friendly interface allows doctors to quickly pull up patient information with less search time and improve doctor–patient dialogue with the avatar as a visualization aid. The end result is more efficient and higher quality patient care.

Customers, too, are a frequent source of ideas and innovations that flow into the firm. For example, a large percentage of the computerized services currently offered by banks were initially self-provided by customers. A detailed description of customer innovations in banking services can be found in Box 5.3. In health care, an international study conducted from 2010 to 2015 found that approximately 1 million individuals had developed medical innovations in the previous 3 years to serve their own needs.[59] Although many of these innovations remain in the public domain for free (e.g., an artificial pancreas for Type 1 diabetes), producers

---

[56]Chesbrough (2011).

[57]IBM (2016a).

[58]IBM (2016b).

[59]DeMonaco et al. (2019).

have refined and commercialized some designs developed by patient innovators. And though most of us think of Legos as a children's toy, a
number of their products are geared toward older users. After initially
being wary of collaboration with customers, the Lego Group eventually
embraced customer collaboration on the design of their products—as
well as customer-driven service innovations such as the websites Auczilla
and BrickLink for buying and selling Lego sets and elements.[60]

Summary: Technology Innovations in the Service Supply Chain

We will revisit many of these technology-enabled service innovations
as we consider how service process design choices and the joint
efforts of service providers and customers co-create value. While these
and other technologies have the potential to deliver faster, better, and
cheaper services, the difficulties supermarkets have faced with self-
service checkouts are instructive examples of unanticipated outcomes.
Likewise, the proliferation of monitoring equipment in the intensive
care unit results in a barrage of beeping and false alarms that may
be tuned out or missed.[61] In a survey of hospitals, clinician desensi-
tization to the constant noise of alarms, termed "alarm fatigue," has
been identified as a top patient safety concern. As for the technologies
that collect customer information, customers may choose not to enter
personal information or enable access to their smartphones via WiFi
or Bluetooth when shopping, for example. But, in reality, customers
are passively providing information about themselves and their actions
constantly through their connected devices, so the days of opting out
of much of this information collection have long passed. Yet these data
collection technologies raise concerns about how personal data is being
used and shared. And now smart devices combine both prolific data
collection and often the disintermediation of humans that changes the
service experience. These examples and concerns highlight the importance of thinking through issues, such as how participants in the service process perceive and use technology, which can point designers

---

[60]Antorini, Muniz, and Askildsen (2012).
[61]MacDonald (2014).

in the right direction when answering the following related questions: How can technology best be integrated into the service process? How does it fit in the overall value co-creation equation?

The Expanded Role of the Customer

When service providers think of the "customer," it is usually as the person or business that is a consumer of its service product. But customers are taking a more active role in the service delivery process itself by performing new tasks or tasks that were previously completed by the service provider. We refer to the joint efforts of the service provider and customer to deliver the service product as "co-production" and the labor contributed by the customer, in particular, as "customer co-production." Customer co-production includes not only physical labor as when pumping gas but also information-based tasks completed by the customer on, for example, e-commerce websites and digital kiosks. These and other SSTs have, to a large extent, enabled the escalating proliferation of customer co-production. Tasks that were formerly the exclusive domain of service providers, such as airport check-in, are now accessible to customers through SSTs. As the availability and profile of these technologies continue to grow and early SST designs are being simplified and updated to improve the customer experience, it is clear that the overall trend toward increasing customer co-production is only going to accelerate. To design service processes so that customers embrace rather than merely accept, or even reject, their expanded role, we need to first understand the customer as a co-producer.

How Customers and Service Providers Differ as Co-Producers

Value co-creation depends on the task performance of both the service provider and the customer. However, service provider and customer co-producers differ in ways that impact the relative effectiveness of their efforts. If we consider customers in their co-producer role as "quasi-employees" of the firm, we can compare the hiring and training of service provider and customer "employees."

Service provider and customer co-producers bring their knowledge, skills, and abilities (KSAs) to the service process tasks. When selecting employees for the firm, the hiring manager naturally chooses individuals with KSAs that meet the task requirements of the job. But this is not as easy—or frequently even possible—to do with customer co-producers. Yet, in knowledge-intensive business services such as consulting, client selection can be critical to service process performance. If client needs fit poorly with consultant KSAs, clients will often be underserviced—resulting in client dissatisfaction—or overserviced—resulting in excessive costs. However, for other services, especially transaction-based services, the criterion for "hiring" a customer is typically the customer's willingness to be "hired"; firms do not usually turn away a willing—and paying—customer, although the idea of "firing" difficult or unprofitable customers has gained some traction.[62] As a result, customer KSAs, as they relate to the co-production tasks, are more variable than those of employees and may not even be relevant to the task at hand.[63] Another important distinction between service provider and customer co-producers is in the amount of control the firm can exert over the actions of its own employees as opposed to its customers. Employees undergo job-related training as a condition of employment and are evaluated on their task performance. Even if customers agree to be "trained" as co-producers—and many opt out altogether—firms have little control over the amount of effort put in and the customer task performance. Although much of this customer training comes in the form of written or verbal directions for customers to follow, some firms are more proactively engaging with customers to help them be better co-producers (Box 2.3).

And, of course, an added complication is the dual roles of the customer—as a consumer of the service product *and* a co-producer in the service process. Unlike actual employees, the service provider does not pay customer co-producers for their efforts—at least not directly. Thus, service providers must have an answer to the customer question, "If I am paying for this service, why should I do (some of) it myself?" In general, the customer needs to perceive benefits of co-production that offset the cost of their labor. In many cases, the customer is indirectly paid for their labor through a price differential (e.g., the telephone booking fee some

---

[62]McGovern (2017).
[63]Frei (2008).

Box 2.3

Customer training to improve service performance

A major public cloud infrastructure service provider conducted a field experiment to determine what effect proactive customer education would have on multiple performance metrics.[64] By offering training on how to use the basic features of the system to a subset of customers who adopted the service during the experiment, the service provider reduced customer churn by half during the first week compared to the control group who did not receive the training, and trained customers asked almost 20 percent fewer questions and increased their total usage of the service by almost 50 percent in the eight 8 months after sign-up. Not surprisingly, these effects were most pronounced for novice customers with no prior experience with the provider, where the training provided the greatest benefit to the customers. Overall, elevating customer capabilities through customer education not only provides revenue and cost advantages to the service provider, but also enables customers to derive more value from services they better understand.

airlines charge for booking a flight by phone rather than online). However, for other services, the benefits are not exclusively or even necessarily monetary. With ATMs and online banking, the convenience of 24/7 banking access and elimination of teller lines compensates customers for their labor. Even without a surcharge for teller transactions, an increasing number of customers *prefer* the ATM and online banking channels over tellers. Contrast this again with the supermarket checkout process, where the self-service channel is the option of last resort for a segment of customers when the full-service lines are too long. How the customer tasks are designed—standardized and simple for the ATM and more complicated and time-consuming for self-service checkout—help determine whether customers will embrace their co-producer role or at best grudgingly accept it.

---

[64]Retana, Forman, and Wu (2016).

Motivating Customer Co-Production

One answer service providers should be able to give to the question of why a paying customer would agree to contribute labor through co-production is, "We have designed service process tasks so you will actually prefer to do them yourself." But before customers can decide that they prefer doing these tasks, the service provider needs to motivate customers to try them out in the first place. Often, this involves guiding customers toward a new self-service delivery channel and providing employee support both for transitioning to self-service and as a safety net if a failure occurs (as supermarkets do by manning a set of checkout kiosks with an employee).[65] However, the motivation for customers to learn about and use self-service may be reduced if they continue to have access to preexisting channels.[66] After all, why make the effort to learn a new system or produce a service independently if it is not necessary—a question that is especially salient for customers who are not comfortable with SSTs or even technology in general?[67]

Studies have shown that customers consider value-based trade-offs when determining whether to take on more co-production tasks. The trade-offs are manifest in questions such as: Do the advantages that customers find in self-service justify their engagement in it? Do customers perceive SSTs to be dependable enough to overcome the uneasiness they feel about their abilities to perform self-service?[68] As the management of the public cloud infrastructure service provider realized when attempting to move more customers to self-service, demonstrating and training customers to use the self-service channel not only signaled the advantages and dependability of SSTs but also reduced customer uneasiness with their own ability to use the technology and helped to break through the inertia.

But getting the customer to perform co-production tasks is not enough. What is even more important is that the customer performs these tasks *well*. And as healthcare processes, such as Sword Health's

---

[65]Kimes and Collier (2015).
[66]Upton and Staats (2008).
[67]Grewal et al. (2020).
[68]Meuter et al. (2005); Looney, Akbulut, and Poston (2008).

physiotherapy at home, are transitioning to include self-service options, concerns about the quality of patient co-production take on added urgency as patients' health or lives can be at stake. Unfortunately, the lack of control over the "hiring" and "training" of customer co-producers can lead to poor quality task performance and the need for additional—and costly—service provider resources such as customer support centers to aid confused customers. Again, customer training helps here, especially when coupled with incentives for better task performance. This can be as simple as conveying to the customer how their efforts affect the service outcomes and their own value realization. Or service providers can incorporate actual rewards (or punishments) to align customer actions with system-level value co-creation. Zipcar,[69] a car sharing service, uses a carrot-and-stick approach to motivating desired customer task performance. They appeal to the customer's sense of community to keep cars in good condition and return them on time. Focusing on the "sharing" part of the service, Zipcar tries to convey how one customer's experience depends on the actions of other customers and appeals to customers to treat others as they would like to be treated themselves. And if that does not work ... late return fees start at $50. Nevertheless, because of the limited control most service providers have over their customers, customer co-producer task performance remains a difficult managerial challenge.

Going back to the issue of customer task design, what else can service providers do to encourage customer co-production? We have already seen that many customers prefer the simple-to-operate ATM over the more complicated supermarket self-service checkout. More generally, customers tend to prefer SSTs when they are perceived as an improvement over the interpersonal alternative, such as gaining increased personal control over the service delivery process. In contrast, customers dislike SSTs when they are poorly designed, including SSTs that are difficult to understand or use.[70]

Ironically, one of the potential pitfalls of even well-designed SSTs is that customers lose sight of the service provider's contribution to value co-creation. In an experiment comparing simulated online travel

---

[69]Zipcar (2020).
[70]Bitner, Ostrom, and Meuter (2002); Montoya-Weiss, Voss, and Grewal (2003).

websites—one with a generic progress bar, one displaying a changing list of which sites were being searched, and one with no delay between clicking the search button and receiving the results—researchers found that people can actually prefer longer waits to instantaneous results, but only if the websites signal effort by listing the airlines being searched.[71] Although each website returned the exact same search results, customers' perceptions of value increased when they felt service providers were doing their fair share of the co-production tasks. I have seen the same dynamic play out in a classroom setting. Students tend to put in more effort when they believe their instructor is working as hard as they are. So perhaps counterintuitively, one way to encourage greater *customer* co-production is to make *service provider* co-production more transparent.

Super-Service

At the same time the general trend is moving toward an expanded role of the customer in the service delivery process, a mirror trend is "super-service."[72] With super-service, the provider performs tasks previously done by the customer. Earlier we saw how the introduction of a self-service channel can help pinpoint how a corresponding full-service channel creates value. The same is true for super-services. For example, Dependable Cleaners,[73] a Boston-based dry cleaner, has complementary home and office pickup and delivery for its dry cleaning service. Although the dry cleaning process itself is unchanged, *access* to the service has moved from self-service to super-service. Dependable Cleaners recognizes that drop-off and pickup are a pain point for many customers. By shifting those "access tasks" to the company, they improve the customer experience and remove a barrier to access, which should translate to more business from these customers.

In addition to the time and effort customers exert to access personal services, the service product itself can be affected by the choice of whether the customer or service provider takes on access tasks. In 2011, Jon Charles Salon introduced "Hairstream," an Airstream trailer converted

---

[71]Buell and Norton (2011).
[72]Campbell, Maglio, and Davis (2011).
[73]Dependable Cleaners (2020).

into a fully equipped mobile hair salon.[74] Not only is it more convenient for time-strapped customers to have stylists travel to their location, but performing the services onsite also eliminates the risk of "damage" to the service product after the customer leaves the salon (e.g., due to the weather). Hairstream's target markets—weddings, proms, special events, and business customers—place a premium on just these attributes. According to Jon Charles, customers also love the "cool" factor—and visibility—of having a high-end hair salon come to them.

Firms like Dependable Cleaners and Jon Charles Salon have made home delivery a core capability and value driver. As part of their value proposition, Dependable Cleaners even promises that their "team of expert garment care professionals develop personal relationships with their clients ... and they become your dedicated point person for all of your laundry and dry cleaning needs."[75] In order to provide efficient and effective service, super-services rely on technologies for scheduling deliveries and managing logistics. As has been the case with self-service, advances in technology have also supported the launch of new super-services (Box 2.4).

Box 2.4

Super-service with remote monitoring

Vendor managed inventory (VMI), in which suppliers manage inventory replenishment on behalf of their customers, is another example of super-service. In the more traditional supply chain model, the customer monitors its own inventory and places an order when necessary. VMI takes these customer tasks and transfers them to the supplier based on the idea that giving the supplier visibility into actual customer demand allows the supply chain to be managed more efficiently and responsively. One of the best- known examples of VMI in retailing is P&G, which manages its in-store inventory for WalMart. In the early days of VMI, a supplier physically monitored their customer's

---

[74]This example is based on an interview with Jon Charles, owner of Jon Charles Salon.
[75]Dependable Cleaners (2020).

inventory levels, but IoT sensor technologies and point-of-sale (POS) data analytics have more recently enabled indirect remote monitoring of inventory. VMI is becoming increasingly common in the grocery industry where margins tend to be thin and inventory management is a key driver of profitability.

Another company making extensive use of remote monitoring for customer service is Ortho-Clinical Diagnostics,[76] a supplier of testing and diagnostics equipment to hospitals, blood banks, and independent labs. Technical support specialists and engineers located in remote monitoring centers use proprietary predictive software to continuously track instruments in the field and identify specific service needs up to 30 days in advance in order to prevent downtime of critical equipment. Despite the potential advantages to the customer of remote services, it is often challenging to convince customers of their value. Unlike onsite customer service, where the customer can see the work being done, remote services are opaque to the customer. In fact, because remote monitoring can be used to provide proactive customer service, the customer may not even know their equipment had been serviced. To raise customer awareness of their value-added remote services, Ortho-Clinical Diagnostics issues a monthly user-value report to each customer reporting the remote services performed.

Summary: Integrating Customers into the Service Process

Customers are moving beyond their role as service consumers to that of co-producers and value co-creators. This requires service providers to think differently about how service process tasks are designed to enable customer co-producers to be effective "quasi-employees" of the firm. More generally, companies should be asking how interactions between the service provider and customer ought to be managed to unlock the value co-creation potential of each party. To start, they need to recognize that service provider and customer co-producers are different in ways that matter with respect to task performance. As a result of these differences, influencing customer actions and task performance continues to be a

---

[76]Ortho-Clinical Diagnostics (2020).

challenge for service process designers. Yet firms such as the public cloud infrastructure service provider in Box 2.3 are figuring it out; they are employing innovative approaches to increasing customer co-production *and* ensuring that customers perform their tasks well.

When all is said and done, for customers to embrace their role as co-producers, they need to believe that the benefits of co-production outweigh the costs of their effort. Service firms can contribute to the customers' perceived value not only by designing tasks and SSTs to be customer-friendly but also by providing incentives for self-service and being a visible partner in the co-production process.

The expanded role of the customer has contributed to changes in the service process design landscape in more ways than one. Although the benefits of self-service have become clearer as customers and firms gain experience with it, the costs have also become more apparent, especially in terms of customer time and effort. Consequently, the limitations of self-service have acted as a catalyst for innovative service delivery models such as "super-service." Taken together, these models—self-service, full-service, and super-service—are providing a broader range of choices for service process design and opportunities for value co-creation.

The Use of Service Inventory

One of the ways in which manufacturing and services are thought to be different is in the presence (manufacturing) or absence (services) of inventory in their production processes. In a manufacturing context, inventory consists of partially or fully completed products built to meet future customer demand. The advantages of inventory include a reduction in time between a customer order and order fulfillment as a supply of the product is already available. In addition, because inventory acts as a buffer between production supply and customer demand, the production schedule can actually be quite smooth and predictable, even if the demand pattern is highly variable. This, in turn, allows operations to be run at higher capacity utilizations and with lower unit costs. But with inventory, as they say, there is no free lunch. Because firms producing to inventory do so before customer-specific demand is known, manufacturers holding inventory risk supply/demand mismatches, with either insufficient supply to meet demand or excess supply of inventory above actual demand.

Unlike manufacturing—where production decisions can be decoupled from demand—customers themselves, their property, and their information are needed for the service process to occur. Take, for example, an auto repair shop. The mechanic can begin work on a customer's car only after it is dropped off at the shop and the problem identified. And, of course, to style a customer's hair, the hairdresser and customer must be co-located. This simultaneity of service production and customer consumption naturally leads to the conclusion that services cannot be inventoried.

However, though we usually associate the term "inventory" with physical goods, it is possible to generalize the concept beyond a manufactured product to "a way to store work." Applying this definition in the manufacturing realm, inventoried goods are simply considered to be the embodiment of stored work. But this opens up the possibility of creating "service inventory," defined as the "portion of the [service] work that has been performed and stored before the customer arrives."[77] As an example of service inventory, the Radian Group of Philadelphia, a title insurance company, collects and stores title information for entire communities prior to any customer-specific demand. This is in contrast to standard industry practice, which is to research a particular property only in response to a customer-initiated request. In every sense, Radian's service inventory fulfills the same purpose as physical goods inventory; it is available to meet immediate customer demand but is created according to Radian's schedule. Radian also bears the risk of insufficient service inventory (demand for properties not in their database) or excess service inventory (no demand for properties that are in their database).

Physical and Digital Service Inventory

Service inventory can take one of two forms: physical or digital. A familiar example of physical service inventory is at the restaurant self-service salad bar. Ingredients are prepared and placed in the salad bar prior to customer demand. Similarly, the lead time would be intolerable if restaurants

---

[77]Chopra and Lariviere (2005) first introduced the concept of "service inventory." The example of the Radian Group is taken from their article.

prepared items such as soup only after a customer order, so soup is made and held in anticipation of customer orders. Clearly, only services that include goods as part of the service product can have physical service inventory. In terms of its advantages and risks, it is indistinguishable from manufacturing product inventory.

In reality, physical service inventory is relatively uncommon for at least two reasons. First, as in the examples of hair styling and auto repair, the customer and customer property, respectively, need to be present for the service process to begin—reducing opportunities to perform and store work before the customer arrives. While the auto repair shop, in particular, often has a significant inventory of tools and parts, this is not what we mean by *service inventory* because none of the service process (repair) work can be done *prior* to the car being onsite. Second, because of the time-sensitive nature of services, the shelf-life of physical service inventory is short. For example, Food and Drug Administration (FDA) regulations limit the time window restaurants have for serving prepared foods. Consequently, the risk—and cost—of excess physical service inventory is high.

But digital service inventory is different, and this is where the power of the service inventory concept is most evident. Take, again, the case of Radian. Undoubtedly, much of the title information Radian collects from entire communities will never be used. But because the process of acquiring information involves transferring data to Radian's electronic database from other electronic databases, the cost of collecting only a few records or thousands of records at a time are practically the same. Although Radian incurred upfront costs to put the data-capture system in place, the incremental cost of any *excess* digital service inventory is virtually zero. Compared with physical service inventory, digital service inventory has the same advantages—quick response to customer demand and smoother and more predictable operations—but with much lower excess costs. Thus, while physical service inventory has limited applicability because of the high cost of unused inventory, opportunities for incorporating digital service inventory in the service process design are growing, enabled by new technologies for capturing, organizing, and analyzing digital content. This is where we will focus our attention.

Three Types of Service Inventory: Undifferentiated Provider-Created, Customer-Specific Co-Created, and Hybrid Customer Class-Specific

Because "service inventory" is a relatively new concept, it makes sense to first look for ideas from manufacturing that can be applied to services. Manufacturing inventory can take a variety of forms, including raw materials, work-in-process (WIP), and finished goods. Producers add value to the product as it moves through the manufacturing process and the work they do is "stored" in partially completed and completed products held in inventory. Although this is similar in many ways to how service inventory is created, we need to also consider how and to what extent customers add value to the service product and the forms in which service inventory is stored. Unlike manufacturing processes, in which producers alone add value and store work, customer inputs are definitionally part of the service process, with customer involvement in creating service inventory ranging from low to high. At the low end of the scale, service inventory is created by the service provider and takes the form of generic or undifferentiated service inventory available to all customers. On the high end of the scale, individual customers are actively involved in creating service inventory to meet their own specific service needs. In the middle of the scale, we find a hybrid form of service inventory available to particular classes of customers that requires some individual customer involvement for determining the class to which they belong. Figure 2.2 shows the positioning of these three types of service inventory in terms of customer involvement in creating the service inventory and the degree of differentiation of the service inventory for different customers. Now let's look in more detail at each type of service inventory.

Undifferentiated Provider-Created Service Inventory

This type of service inventory is "created by the service provider in anticipation of customer demand but is not customized for a specific consumer."[78] The defining characteristics of undifferentiated provider-created service inventory are that it is the same for all customers and individual

---

[78]Davis, Field, and Stavrulaki (2015).

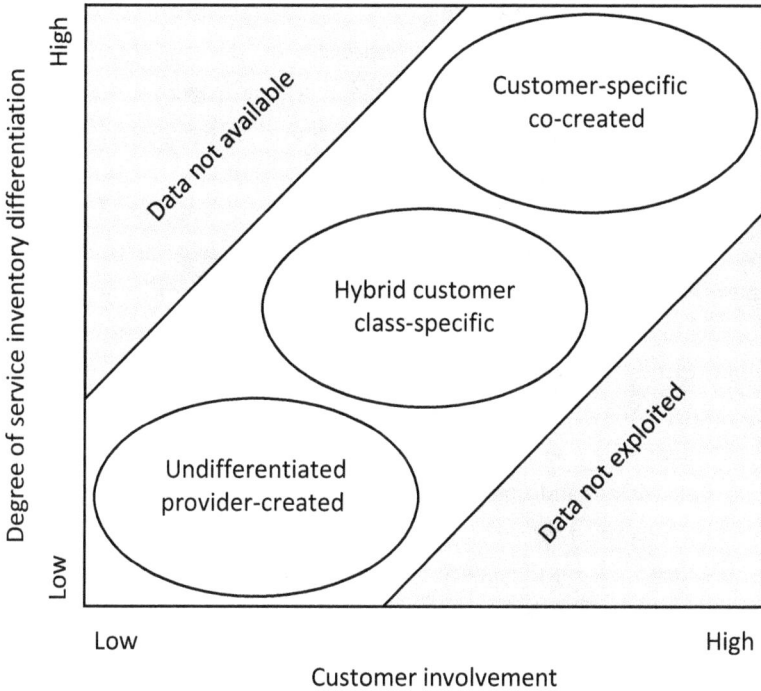

Figure 2.2 *Building digital service inventory with customer involvement*

customers are not directly involved in its creation (i.e., it is positioned in the lower left corner of Figure 2.2). Examples include stored information on financial products and analytical tools on Google Finance, information on medical conditions on the WebMD site, information on products and product availability on online grocery websites, and airfare and seat availability on airline websites—all in a searchable format. Certain user-generated content can also be considered this type of service inventory, but only to the extent that it is collected by the provider and made available to all customers. The ubiquitous customer reviews on e-commerce sites are an example—a customer uses the review information gathered from *other* customers as part of their own purchase process. Each of these qualifies as undifferentiated provider-created service inventory because the information is collected and the analytical and search task capabilities are developed and made available—by the provider with no differentiation by customer—prior to the customer entering the service system. In other words, this is "stored work" that would otherwise need to be performed during the service delivery process.

Although the focus here is on digital service inventory, it is worth noting that examples of undifferentiated provider-created service inventory do exist in the physical realm as well—and not only at salad bars. Although the cost of excess physical service inventory limits its use in most service processes, pairing it with information technology can help reduce the risk by better matching the amount of service inventory and its positioning in the process relative to demand. Dell knows that in the event of a hurricane or other severe weather, customers tend to power-down their computers. When powered-up again, historical data show a five to seven times increase in power supply and hard drive failures. Recognizing this, Dell prepositions additional power supplies and hard drives based on the weather forecast in the areas expected to be affected. By shipping parts to where they are likely to be needed *before* they are needed, Dell is building service inventory for use by any of its customers.

Customer-Specific Co-Created Service Inventory

In contrast to undifferentiated provider-created service inventory, customer-specific co-created service inventory is—as its name suggests—specific to individual customers and co-created through the collaborative efforts of the customer and provider. This type of service inventory can be built in a number of ways. One approach is picking and choosing elements of the undifferentiated provider-created service inventory to construct personalized service inventory. This is similar to the assemble-to-order process popularized by Dell, in which customized computers are produced by mixing and matching standard components (e.g., processor, memory storage, screen). Going back to the example of Google Finance, as customers assemble their personal financial portfolios from the undifferentiated service inventory of financial products and analytical tools stored by Google, they are initially co-creating a customer-specific product. The work of entering account and portfolio information is stored on Google's server and is available to customers for tracking their portfolio performance, without having to provide the same information a second time. By doing so, the service product becomes "customer-specific co-created" service inventory for subsequent dealings with Google. And the customer can continue to individualize their service experience with updates to their financial portfolio. Similarly, customers can generate their family's grocery lists from the generic product and product availability information on online grocery websites. These grocery lists can then be saved as customer-specific service inventory for future orders.

In a second approach, customers interact with the service provider, either interpersonally or through technologies, and actively or passively provide information about themselves that can be used to create customer-specific service inventory. This can be as straightforward as actively storing their shipping address and credit card information with an online retailer for future transactions. Or customers may passively provide information in the form of "data exhaust," which is the unintentional by-product of customer interactions. For example, website click patterns can be tracked while customers shop online, and this data can be stored as service inventory to guide future search results for individual customers. Customers on the dating apps mentioned earlier co-create personalized service inventory both actively and passively— actively when they set up their profiles and preferences and passively when they swipe right or left. The apps' AI algorithms learn from a customer's swiping pattern to present dating options better aligned with these implied preferences.

As new technologies for capturing customer information are being deployed in service processes, and firms are getting better at making sense of the volume and variety of the data being collected, opportunities to build even more customized service inventory are increasing. Recall that Apple Maps suggests a travel route based on data generated by a person's smartphone, creating an individualized customer experience. Rather than a service delivery process that starts only after customer demand is known, this is instead a process in which the firm predicts what the customer will want based on previous interactions and then does the work of producing the service product ahead of customer demand. Yet this highly customer-specific service inventory is truly co-created due to the tight linkage between customer-provided information and the efforts of the service provider. But what if the customer does not want to take the travel route suggested by Apple Maps? Although it goes to "waste," the *marginal* cost of creating it through an automated process is minimal and thus the excess service inventory cost is small.

The same principle applies when interactions with the customer are interpersonal instead of through a technology. For the Ritz-Carlton, important data sources for its "Mystique" CRM system are staff observations about guests. As an example, a couple vacationing at a Ritz-Carlton in Cancun found their room temperature to be too warm—with the problem persisting even after the thermostat was replaced. The concierge showed the couple two other rooms, one that was cooler and one that had a nicer view, with the couple choosing the cooler room. The couple's preference for a cool room—even one with an inferior view—was noted in the Mystique system. Although the Ritz-Carlton would attempt to provide both in any subsequent stay, a cool room would now be the first priority.[79] This information is service inventory for the Ritz-Carlton, as it reduces the work to collect customer-specific information to meet that customer's subsequent service needs.

Of course, if the firm does a poor job of anticipating customer demand in the aggregate, its collection of individualized service inventory is of little value. But the more times customers interact with the firm, the more likely the firm will get it right much of the time. The ProAir Digihaler asthma and COPD management system mentioned earlier is a good example of how this can work. The more data ProAir Digihaler collects on a patient, the better it is at identifying patterns; whether it is an unusually frequent use of a rescue inhaler or daily self-assessments of how the patient feels, the usefulness of individualized service inventory for managing a patient's asthma or COPD improves as the patient continues to use the product. Similarly, the more metrics and data points Ortho-Clinical Diagnostics collects and stores from a piece of equipment in a hospital, blood bank, or independent lab, the more accurately it can diagnose a problem. The database and diagnostic tools qualify as service inventory because the work is done before the customer contacts the firm for service. This enables quicker response to potential equipment failures and more predictable scheduling of onsite technicians if needed.

---

[79]Blandino (2016).

Going forward, the explosive growth of smart devices—with their extensive data collection and analysis capabilities—means that service inventory will play an even more prominent role in service delivery processes. Thus, the design of smart device service inventory—including, what information to collect, what triggers a service response—is central to whether and how value is created. For example, smart cushions on wheelchairs can notify healthcare providers when patients are at risk of pressure sores and respond before patients even realize there is a problem.[80] The virtual fitness coaches mentioned earlier can collect and analyze customer fitness metrics to create service inventory used to design individualized training plans. Designed properly, personal care service inventory based on smart device data will "spot the complex trends and interactions that no one could detect alone [and] pre-empt many illnesses."[81]

Hybrid Customer Class-Specific Service Inventory

In the middle of Figure 2.2, we find examples such as Samsung monitoring social media (Facebook, Twitter, Instagram) and other customer feedback channels for early signs of product problems. The firm then proactively pushes information and solutions to customers who own these products. Because the work of building solutions is done before most customers even know there is an issue, this is service inventory. It is co-created by Samsung engineers and an *aggregation* of numerous customers providing feedback as opposed to a high level of *individual* customer interaction. Additionally, it is specific to a *class* of customers owning the affected product but not to an individual customer, so it falls between undifferentiated and customer-specific service inventory. We term this "hybrid customer class-specific" service inventory.

Contrast this with "collaborative filtering," a statistical technique underlying Netflix's and Amazon's recommendation systems, which makes user-specific recommendations based on each user's similarity to other users and their preferences. Netflix's system uses machine-learning and clustering techniques to divide its more than 130 million global members

---

[80]Predix (2016).
[81]Topol (2015).

into over 1,000 "taste communities."[82] An individual customer's affinity with one or more taste communities drives movie recommendations based on subjects popular with the communities. While Samsung, Netflix, and Amazon are all aggregating information across many customers, the focus of collaborative filtering is on how an individual customer relates to a class of customers. And as individual customers repeatedly interact with Netflix or Amazon, the additional information collected results in an increasingly fine-tuned understanding of their customer class similarities and targeted recommendations (i.e., product search "work" done before the next customer transaction).

In an example of pairing physical service inventory with information technology that qualifies as hybrid customer class-specific service inventory, the UK-based retailer Tesco collects detailed information on customers who use their loyalty cards (including which stores customers visit) to adjust product offerings by store to match local tastes. The "class" of customers are those who shop at each store and the service inventory is the assortment of products predetermined through the aggregation of data on their shopping patterns.

Referring back to Figure 2.2, as we move from undifferentiated provider-created to hybrid customer class-specific to customer-specific co-created service inventory, the digital service inventory becomes increasingly customized for individual customers. And as service inventory becomes even more individualized as customers repeatedly interact with the firm, customer loyalty also increases. This is due to the cost of switching to another firm and recreating the entire customer profile of information collected both actively and passively. For example, in addition to the effort to set up an account and put together a shopping list after downloading a retailer's app, the app collects search and purchasing history and uses it to offer targeted coupons, accrue loyalty points, and make the shopping experience more efficient.[83] As a result, customers are more likely to stay with the current service provider as long as their service needs are being met.

---

[82]Lee and Shin (2020).
[83]Edmund (2015).

Two undesirable positions in Figure 2.2 are also worth noting. In the upper left corner of the diagram is the position, "Data not available"; a low level of customer interaction provides limited data for moving beyond undifferentiated to customer-specific service inventory. Being in the "Data not exploited" lower right corner indicates that the service provider either did not collect available customer data or did not use the data effectively to co-create customer-specific service inventory. We will come back later to the question of what firms can do to improve the value equation if they find themselves in either of these two positions.

Much of the information captured for building customer-specific service inventory also supports personalized marketing efforts using CRM databases.[84] By analyzing the data that is collected about or provided by their customers, firms can target marketing efforts to individuals or groups of customers based on personal characteristics and history with the company.[85] Organizations with an online channel have an advantage over pure brick-and-mortar players in this regard. Not only can they collect information from customer purchases and surveys, but they also have access to customer data from everything that happens on their sites. For example, before rolling out a new feature, Internet companies can run a smaller-scale experiment and refine the feature based on customer click behavior and other feedback.[86] Best-practice firms such as Amazon, eBay, and especially Google, generate tremendous economic value from mining customer data to improve their service process design.[87] Leveraging this customer information for *operational benefits* in addition to marketing purposes has become an important source of competitive advantage in the marketplace.

When Is Service Inventory Most Valuable?

When deciding what type of service inventory, if any, to include in the service process design, the key consideration is how it contributes to value co-creation. Does it decrease costs, reduce service delivery time, or

---

[84]Davenport, Dalle Mule, and Lucker (2011).
[85]Rust and Verhoef (2005).
[86]"Clicking for Gold" (2010).
[87]Ibid.

improve the customer experience? And under what conditions are these favorable outcomes most likely to occur? To answer these questions, let's focus on three factors—demand volume, repeatability, and service inventory positioning—that impact service inventory costs, benefits, or both.

Demand Volume

Although the marginal cost of creating an incremental unit of digital service inventory is low, firms incur upfront costs for developing the databases and tools that comprise undifferentiated, hybrid, and customer-specific service inventory. Because much of the cost of creating service inventory is fixed—at least in the short term—the *average* unit cost of service inventory is related to the demand volume. In other words, the greater the customer demand for service products using service inventory, the lower the average cost due to economies of scale. Ideally, the customer-perceived value of service inventory drives higher demand and this extra demand further decreases average cost and drives even higher demand. Of course, high upfront costs for service inventory increases the firm's risk if the expected demand fails to materialize, making it especially critical to define and communicate its value to the customer.

Repeatability

As a customer repeatedly uses a service—for example, shopping at Amazon or staying at the Ritz-Carlton multiple times—the value of their customer-specific service inventory increases for at least two reasons: First, repeatability impacts the probability that customer-specific service inventory will actually be used. If a customer enters and stores their shipping address and credit card information on an e-tailer's website, this customer-specific service inventory will only be used if the customer transacts with the company again. Second, repeat demand for a service by an individual customer expands the opportunities for the service provider to gather additional customer information. Consequently, the quality and range of the customer-specific service inventory improves as more comprehensive customer information is available. This has a positive impact on the service provider's ability to anticipate the individual customer's service need and proactively provide services. Both Amazon's recommendation system and the Ritz-Carlton's Mystique system better predict customer needs with fuller information about the customer. The same is true for service inventory built through smart devices.

Service Inventory Positioning

In the digital service inventory examples in this section, the methods for creating service inventory are highly automated with little or no manual co-productive effort after the initial systems development (although as the Ritz-Carlton example demonstrates, service inventory co-creation may also include information collected through the provider's interactions with customers). But because the amount of service work that can be done ahead of time varies from process to process, the rest of the service process involves additional service provider or customer effort. Thus, the *positioning* of service inventory in the process determines the amount of work left to be done to complete the service. On the one end of the service inventory continuum are "reactive" processes (no service inventory, with the entire service product produced after the customer enters the service system); on the other end are "proactive" processes (a complete service product produced to forecasted customer demand). "Mixed" processes, with a combination of service inventory and service tasks to be completed after the customer enters the service system, are positioned somewhere between these endpoints. Following are two examples of mixed processes. The financial products and analytical tools on Google Finance are prepositioned undifferentiated inventory, with customer-specific service inventory (individual portfolios) created by each customer during the service process. Radian's title insurance process is a variant of this in which Radian employees access their service inventory of title information and complete the service process after receiving a customer order. Apple Maps, in comparison, pushes service inventory all the way to the customer by suggesting travel routes—the complete service product—in a proactive process. Figure 2.3 shows the positioning of service inventory in a mixed process. The vertical lines at each end denote the beginning and end of the service process. The downward arrow indicates the point at

Customer
enters service
system

Service inventory   Additional service tasks
created in antici-   completed and service
pation of customer   inventory used
needs

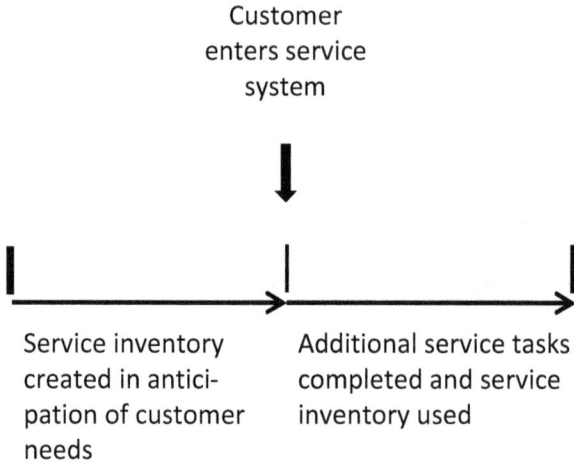

Figure 2.3 *Positioning of service inventory in a mixed service process*

which the customer enters the service system. All process tasks to the right are completed after the customer enters and all process tasks to the left (i.e., service inventory) are completed before the customer enters the service system. In contrast, in a reactive process, the customer enters at the beginning of the process and all tasks are completed with the customer in the service system. A proactive process uses service inventory only and the customer does not enter the service system until the end of the process.

As with other service process design decisions, it is important to consider how service inventory creates value for the different service participants. Unlike the mostly automated processes for undifferentiated provider-created service inventory, customers themselves provide personal information and often assemble customer-specific service inventory. So for the service provider, the positioning of service inventory is largely a technology investment decision. But from the customer's perspective, the main question is whether the benefits of service inventory outweigh the costs in terms of their time and effort. Included in the customer's cost assessment is their willingness to share personal information—either actively or passively through provider technologies. As with supermarket self-service checkout kiosks, service provider and customer perspectives on the relative benefits and costs of service inventory often diverge. This can be an especially sensitive issue when it involves collecting and storing customer information and positioning it in the process as service inventory. Privacy concerns, such as potential identity theft, are a "cost" incurred primarily by the customer (although, relatedly, data breeches have direct and reputational costs to the service provider as well). As a result, when their privacy costs are high, customers value this service inventory less than service providers—even if that means their personal information must be reentered with each subsequent transaction. Customer and service provider perspectives clearly need to be reconciled when determining whether and how to include service inventory in the service process design.

Summary: Incorporating Service Inventory into the Service Process

Although the concept of "service inventory" is relatively new, physical versions of it have been around for a long time. Anytime restaurant-goers assemble salads from a self-service salad bar or order soup from the menu, they are eating food that was at least partially prepared before they sat down. But when pre-producing to forecasted customer demand in the physical realm, the cost of excess inventory can be sizable if it ends up going to waste due to a mismatch with actual customer demand. Additionally, with the highly variable demand that is characteristic of service processes, the risk and cost of excess physical service inventory can be prohibitive. However, with advances in information technology, the real potential for using service inventory in the service delivery process lies in the creation of *digital* service inventory. Although firms incur substantial upfront costs putting systems in place to collect data from service suppliers and customers to build undifferentiated and customer-specific service inventory, the marginal cost of excess service inventory is low. By virtually eliminating this downside of holding inventory—and assuming sufficient customer demand to defray the fixed costs—firms now have another powerful tool in their service process design toolkit.

We have covered examples of firms using remote monitoring to build a database and predict pending equipment failures before the customer even suspects a problem. Other firms are mining social media—or weather reports—to proactively solve problems. Customer information stored in call center support systems are moving contact centers into "relationship" centers as these systems enable the service experience to become increasingly individualized with repeated customer interactions. All of these involve completing and storing service process work *before* the customer enters the service system. These examples demonstrate how the judicious positioning of service inventory, coupled with additional service provider and customer co-productive efforts, can contribute to faster, better, and cheaper services.

CHAPTER 3

Value Co-Creation in Service Processes

Simply put, the goal of service process design is to provide a mechanism for unlocking value co-creation. We now focus on the question of how to do this—how to bring service providers and customers together through the service process design to co-create value. Clearly, technology-enabled service innovations, the expanded role of the customer, and the use of service inventory are part of the answer; we have presented a number of examples demonstrating their impact on service process design. These factors have figured and will continue to figure prominently in the emerging service process landscape as service providers and customers demand ever greater value from services.

Before continuing, let's return to the definitions of value and value co-creation from Chapter 1 and reexamine them in more detail, and then proceed to determine exactly what it is that is being "unlocked." Recall that value is created when benefits are perceived to be greater than the costs of obtaining those benefits. Even though services that do not provide value to *all* participants cannot survive in the long term, neither the service provider nor the customer create value in a vacuum. Instead, the value that each party gains from a service is dependent, to a large degree, on their interactions with other parties. As we have seen, these interactions may be person-to-person but can also occur between a service provider and a customer's property and information or between a customer and a self-service technology. Regardless of the nature of the interactions, this interdependence means that value is *co-created* through the collaborative activities of the service provider and customer and the integration of their labor, capital, and information resources.[1] But as we saw in Chapter 1, customers and service providers may have very different perspectives regarding the benefits and costs of a particular service. And, as illustrated by the ongoing challenges with supermarket self-service checkout, failure to fully consider the actual drivers of value across all parties can result in a less-than-optimal service process design.

So to unlock value, we need to understand what the benefits, costs, and value calculations are from the perspectives of both the customer and the service provider. Building on the ideas in Chapter 1 for ATMs and self-service checkout kiosks, we now develop a more complete set of benefits and costs from which customers and service providers calculate value.

Value from the Customer's Perspective

Customers buy services to meet their needs, and they judge the value of the service based on how well their needs are met relative to the costs incurred. For business-to-customer (B2C) services, customers make this judgment on their own behalf. However, for business-to-business (B2B) services, customers not only care how well their business needs are being met but also whether these services help them to better meet the needs of their own customers. But what specific criteria do customers use to gauge the benefits and costs that comprise "value"? In a competitive environment, firms differentiate and customers evaluate services based not only on price but also on delivery speed, quality, flexibility, and innovation. Let's look at each of these dimensions in more detail.

Dimensions of Customer Benefits

From the customers' perspective, the most easily quantifiable measure included in their value calculation is the price of the service—and all else being equal, the lower the better. Although firms can charge low prices in the short term regardless of their actual cost structure, long-term sustainability of the business requires low prices to be supported by low costs for the service delivery process itself. Delivery speed is similarly

---

[1]Oertzen et al. (2018).

straightforward; fast delivery compresses the time between the start and end of the service process.

Service quality, in contrast, is much more complex and consists of multiple subdimensions. The general consensus is that service quality has five subdimensions: reliability (the service is performed dependably and accurately); responsiveness (service providers are willing to help customers, provide prompt service, and recover quickly from service failures); assurance (service providers are knowledgeable and courteous and convey trust and confidence); empathy (service providers are caring and treat customers as individuals); and tangibles (the physical environment and materials—facilities, equipment, personnel—are appropriate).[2] These subdimensions are focused on how the customer experiences the service and include both technical outcomes (was the service performed accurately?), as well as the emotional and psychological impact on the customer (do customers have a sense of trust and confidence in the service provider?) and were originally developed for services where the service provider and customer interact directly. Subsequently, a set of service quality subdimensions was developed specifically for e-commerce.[3] They closely parallel the ones above, with "website design" substituting for "tangibles." Because of the online delivery channel, data security and privacy is a quality subdimension particular to e-commerce, and more broadly, to any services that collect and store customer data. Data security and privacy are becoming increasingly critical quality concerns as firms are gathering a greater volume and variety of customer information, some of which is highly sensitive, such as health and financial data. And regardless of whether a service is delivered in-person, online, or by other technologies, convenient or "frictionless" services that incorporate elements from all of the quality subdimensions have become the holy grail for customers and service providers.[4] However, in Box 3.1, we will see some of the unexpected trade-offs in pursuit of the frictionless ideal.

---

[2]Parasuraman, Zeithaml, and Berry (1988).
[3]Wolfinbarger and Gilly (2003).
[4]Grewal et al. (2020).

Box 3.1

The trade-offs in "frictionless" services[5]

Rising customer expectations for services that are easier and less time-consuming to navigate have prompted providers to respond by introducing new service processes or redesigning existing processes to remove frictions that slow them down or make them more difficult. For example, social media platforms such as Facebook and Twitter allow users to easily message to huge audiences; using collaborative filtering-based service inventory, YouTube's auto-play function selects a new video to start as soon as the previous one is done. Probably the best known frictionless service is one-click ordering, introduced by Amazon in the 1990s. In many ways, these sound like they should be "model" services from the customer's perspective—low cost, fast delivery, high quality, and in many cases flexible and innovative as well. But even frictionless services involve trade-offs; making these services so easy to use creates security vulnerabilities, which can result in devastating outcomes such as identity theft. To manage the trade-off between frictionlessness and data security, providers are reintroducing frictions into these services, for example, security Captchas and two-step verifications.

Another less obvious trade-off involves how customers value certain frictionless services. For example, as a new start-up, Tulerie, a platform that allows women to share designer clothing, e-mailed out a brief Google survey to hundreds of women to assess its market potential. But only one woman actually filled out the survey. After the failure of this low friction tactic, the founders pivoted to a more complicated approach requiring anyone who wanted to join the platform to have a video call with an employee first. Unexpectedly, this was a big hit, with the company's interview schedule filling up weeks in advance. It turns out that by making the Tulerie sign-up process frictionless, potential customers did not place a high value on the service. However, making it more difficult "signaled that its service was special and worth the effort."

---

[5]The examples in this box are from Roose (2018).

Paradoxically, when technology mediates the interaction between the customer and service provider, designing service processes to meet the customer's emotional and psychological needs may actually be more critical to the customer's perception of service quality. The lack of direct service provider-to-customer contact creates a barrier to the real-time adjustments that employees can make to accommodate specific customer needs. In fact, customer frustration with poorly designed e-commerce sites results in overall negative perceptions of the service experience—even if the rest of the process (e.g., product delivery) is perfect.[6] This is why many firms now monitor their websites to proactively intervene with a live employee to help customers who appear to be having difficulties or questions and turn what could be a negative service experience into a positive one. This live chat creates something termed a "social presence,"[7] which is the felt presence of others, that many customers miss in a pure technology-mediated service. However, the emotional and psychological benefits of social presence can be achieved through other service process design choices as well, including posts by other customers, video chat with a friend while shopping, or interactions with conversational agent technologies such as Alexa or Siri.

For services that do include provider-to-customer contact, the increasing use of artificial intelligence (AI) to perform not only mechanical and repetitive work but also analytical and thinking tasks elevates the importance of the "empathy" subdimension and puts a premium on the interpersonal and emotional capabilities of employees. This shift toward a "Feeling Economy,"[8] in which employees' primary job responsibilities involve people-focused tasks, is redefining how firms hire and train employees and how the quality of customer service is assessed. As an example of the growing emphasis on these subjective aspects of quality, recall from Box 2.2 that call centers are increasingly using AI-based products such as Cogito to both evaluate and coach their employees on interpersonal skills and emotional intelligence.

---

[6]Bitner, Ostrom, and Meuter (2002).
[7]Grewal et al. (2020).
[8]Huang, Rust, and Maksimovic (2019).

Flexibility is about customer choice—the range of services offered, the degree of customization allowed, and the types of delivery channels available (online, offline, kiosks, etc.). For example, Small Luxury Hotels (SLH) of the World, an affiliation of over 500 small hotels across 80 countries, offers a wide range of experiences to its guests.[9] Their properties range from historic mansions to a cave resort and spa, with the spirit of all hotels in the SLH group embodied in their tagline: "independently minded." Each hotel "offer[s] a unique personal touch that leaves a lasting impression," supported by customer-specific service inventory in the form of a personal profile of stay preferences entered online by the customer. And in omni-channel models, service firms are providing more choices of service delivery channels—both physical and digital—to create a seamless experience.[10] Although retailers and other omni-channel businesses offer increased flexibility with more service delivery channel options, many still struggle with integrating the channels to ensure a consistent customer experience (e.g., pricing and customer engagement) across channels and to create a truly integrated value chain.

Service innovation is the introduction of new service products or delivery processes that better meet existing customer needs or meet new (and often previously unknown) customer needs. Smart services and other technology-enabled service innovations described earlier certainly qualify under this definition. For example, in the realm of e-commerce, MTailor is a men's clothing e-tailer that takes customer measurements using a smartphone camera.[11] A customer simply places their phone on the floor against a wall and turns around once, providing MTailor with all the sizing information it needs to create custom suits, shirts, pants and jeans. MTailor and other e-tailers also serve as repositories for customer-specific information that functions as service inventory for subsequent transactions. As another example, Bloomberg terminals have revolutionized the way financial professionals access and analyze data. The service innovation is not the data itself; most of the information available on a "Bloomberg" is publicly available. Rather, it

---

[9]Small Luxury Hotels of the World (2020).
[10]Weill and Woerner (2015).
[11]MTailor (2020).

is the aggregation of data and news from numerous sources, real-time accessibility through the terminal, and the built-in analytical tools that constitute the service innovation. Even at a price of up to $24,000 per user per year, over 325,000 customers use Bloomberg's terminal service.[12] In addition to service innovations that better meet existing customer needs, social networking services such as Facebook and Twitter are meeting needs no one could have imagined even existed in the not-too-distant past.

The Inevitability of Making Trade-Offs

Even though it may seem that the "model" service firm would offer the lowest costs, fastest delivery, highest quality, greatest flexibility, and most innovative services simultaneously, unfortunately this isn't possible. Excellence in one dimension typically comes at the expense of other dimensions, which is why we see firms in the same industry appealing to different customer segments and needs.[13] For example, Jiffy Lube (and other firms such as Valvoline Instant Oil Change) focuses very narrowly—primarily on oil changes—within the car maintenance industry. Consequently, the service process design is highly standardized, with every aspect optimized to quickly and efficiently perform oil changes. What they don't offer is a wide range of other car maintenance services. But for customers who only want a quick, inexpensive oil change without an appointment, Jiffy Lube is just the ticket.

Benefits for the customer are lower costs and faster service time than at a car dealership service department or independent auto service shop. However, the inability to handle a wider range of car maintenance needs is a potential "cost" (e.g., if the customer has to make multiple trips to different service providers). Because of trade-offs among cost, quality, delivery speed, flexibility, and innovation, firms in this and other industries position their services differently (e.g., low cost and fast delivery for Jiffy Lube versus greater flexibility at a car dealership). Therefore, each customer makes a decision where to go for car maintenance based on their

---

[12]Wall Street Prep (2020).
[13]Frei (2008).

own value determination (benefits less costs) to meet their particular service needs.

In other words, the existence of trade-offs requires customers to decide what most matters to them. Clearly, the services provided by hotels affiliated with SLH cost more than those at the lower-end Motel 6. In addition to the higher quality of the "tangibles" at SLH, customized services are simply more expensive to provide than standardized ones. Much of the difference in cost is due to the labor-intensive—and therefore, costly—interactions between the service provider and customer. These interactions are needed to determine customization requirements and to manage any ongoing involvement of the customer (e.g., redefining requirements as the service process goes along). Financial planners and their customers know this trade-off well; the more individualized a financial plan, the more time, effort, and costs are involved. The examples could go on and on (e.g., Amazon customers trade-off cost and delivery by paying for an Amazon Prime membership for faster delivery), but the point is that making trade-offs is an inherent part of service process design.

Softening the Trade-Offs

However, we also know that service processes can be designed to mitigate some of these trade-offs. Remote monitoring technologies more quickly and accurately diagnose impending equipment failures and fix problems before customers are even aware of them. Compared with the usual process of contacting the vendor after an equipment failure, who then dispatches a repair technician to the customer's site, "delivery speed" is faster with the same quality (and arguably better quality if the timing of the problem resolution—before versus after equipment failure—is taken into account). Similarly, other smart devices, such as the virtual fitness coaches and wheelchair smart cushions from Chapter 2, use sense and respond capabilities and customer-specific service inventory to provide both faster and higher quality services.

Trader Joe's, a specialty grocery chain, is another example of a firm making process design choices that reduce the trade-offs customers experience.[14] While Trader Joe's smaller stores have a narrower product range than a typical grocery store (4,000 stock-keeping units [SKUs] versus 50,000 SKUs), each product is carefully chosen as a best-in-category, so quality is high. But Trader Joe's is also able to keep costs down—despite the small store size—by putting its stores in low-cost locations (often strip malls), with distribution economies from buying directly from the manufacturer (80 percent of their products are Trader Joe's branded), and through the purchasing power afforded by its narrow product range (it buys more of fewer items). By lowering costs throughout its supply chain, Trader Joe's can attract and pay employees for outstanding service while keeping its prices competitive with larger chains.

When it comes to quality versus cost, service process designers are finding opportunities for inexpensively improving quality. Engineers know that for manufactured products, redundant components can be designed into the product (e.g., back-up power sources for pacemakers) to improve reliability. Similarly, redundant systems can be designed into service processes. For example, due to the use of multiple redundant systems, including computers and utilities, trading on the New York Stock Exchange (NYSE) continued uninterrupted during and after the August 23, 2011, earthquake on the east coast.[15] But these types of solutions are an expensive way to go. Obviously, for critical products like pacemakers—and the trading operations of the NYSE—redundancies make sense. However, in many situations—even for truly critical services like surgery—reliability can sometimes be improved with little or no increase in cost. We already saw this with the data-matrix-coded sponge (DMS) system in place in the Mayo Clinic Rochester operating rooms. With little additional cost and virtually no additional time and effort by the OR personnel, the rate of retained sponges has come down to zero. We can also find examples of decidedly low-tech initiatives that are having a significant impact on OR quality. Inspired by pilot checklists that have been in use in the

---

[14]Kowitt (2010).
[15]McDougall (2011).

airline industry for decades, the implementation of simple checklists in operating rooms around the world has dramatically improved the safety of surgical procedures.[16] With simple yes or no questions about, for instance, patient allergies, antibiotics given, and introduction of all surgical team members to each other, the checklist takes less than 2 minutes to complete. Design choices such as these illustrate that it is often possible to significantly lessen the extent of trade-offs and increase the value customers perceive from the service process.

Costs of Customer Time and Effort

To further fill in our list of benefits and costs to the customer, we now return to the cost side of the value equation. With the trend toward an expanded role of the customer in service processes, the question of how customers value their time and effort merits further consideration. In addition to the price, the costs customers attribute to their time and effort are part of their overall value calculation that drives the choice of whether to purchase a service and, if so, through which delivery channel. All else being equal, we expect customers with high-perceived time and effort costs to prefer full-service or super-service and value a frictionless service experience regardless of the service delivery model. For example, recognizing that many people do not have time to spend shopping at car dealerships but like the idea of personal service, a former car salesman started his own car-buying "concierge" service that handles the selection, negotiation, purchase, and delivery of cars to customers on a commission basis.[17] This frictionless super-service, advertised exclusively through word of mouth, has clearly found a market with time-strapped customers—his sales range up to 52 cars per month.

But, of course, customers do not consider these costs in isolation. Rather, they are combined with other costs and benefits, some of which involve trade-offs with their own time and effort (Box 3.2).

---

[16]Gawande (2010).
[17]Howard (2020).

Box 3.2

Incorporating customer waiting time into value calculations

The following two studies show just how expensive customer waiting time really is. Based on respondent-reported costs for their own time, TOA Technologies "Cost of Waiting" survey[18] estimates an economic impact of over $37 billion each year in the United States from customers waiting for scheduled in-home services—the equivalent of removing the average American from the workforce for two full days per year. A study in the fast-food drive-thru industry[19] goes one step further and calculates the cost of customer waiting using data based on actual customer behavior during the service process rather than customer-reported costs. The results of the study suggest that an additional *second* in the drive-thru line requires compensation in the form of a $0.05 reduction in the price of the meal that typically goes for only $2.50 to $6. This corresponds to a valuation put on customer waiting time of approximately $180 per hour or 10 times the average wage of $18 per hour in Illinois, where the study was conducted. In fact, the authors of the study conclude that "waiting time plays a more significant role than pricing in explaining sales volume." This also implies that investments to reduce waiting time by firms in the industry should pay off through higher customer demand while, at the same time, allowing the firms to maintain its pricing levels.

Even the Registry of Motor Vehicles (RMV)—not usually known as the paragon of customer service—has redesigned its services to reduce customer waiting time.[20] Changes at the RMV include,

increasing the use of existing alternative service channels, increasing RMV staff performance measured by improving accountability and customer treatment, and improving customer wait times through the use of dual queuing methods that have eliminated

---

[18]TOA Technologies (2011). TOA Technologies was acquired by Oracle in 2014.
[19]Allon, Federgruen, and Pierson (2011).
[20]Mass.Gov (2016).

hidden wait times at participating branches. The RMV has also redesigned MassRMV.com to be more customer friendly and improved outreach to increase online use.

In fact, the RMV encourages customers to go online using self-service for over 20 services, including license renewal, scheduling a branch appointment, ordering a Fast Lane transponder, and canceling a registration plate. Customers can also sign up online for a free license renewal or Massachusetts ID reminder service. For customers who still need to visit a branch or prefer services through the branch channel, the RMV expanded their hours in 2011 at several of its busiest branch locations to reduce waiting times. A better match of capacity to demand and other process changes at the branches have paid off: "The RMV served 87% of customers in under 30 minutes in 2019 surpassing the wait time target of 80%. This wait time improvement represents a 17% increase in the RMV's ability to serve customers under 30 minutes from 2018."[21] All of these initiatives—as well as posting branch waiting times online—are acknowledgments that customer waiting at RMV branches exacts a high cost from the customer's perspective. But why should a "monopoly" like the RMV care about reducing customer waiting times and improving the customer experience when customers have nowhere else to go for these services? The answer lies in understanding how benefits from the customer's perspective can create synergies from the service provider's perspective. This idea will be developed in more detail shortly.

Summary: Customer-Perceived Value and Service Process Design

When thinking about the set of benefits and costs for calculating value from the customer's perspective, it is important to keep two points in mind. First, even though the potential benefits include low cost, high quality, fast delivery, flexibility, and innovation, trade-offs mean that each of these can also be on the cost side of the value equation—as we saw with flexibility being sacrificed for low cost and fast delivery at Jiffy Lube. Second, a number of factors can impact the customer's assessment of the

---

[21]Pollack (2019).

service experience—and these assessments will vary by customer. With regard to the value of digital customer-specific service inventory, for example, individual customers will evaluate the costs associated with data security and privacy differently and weigh these self-determined costs against the benefits (e.g., faster delivery). The same is true for the costs of customer waiting time and effort. Some customers value the control they have with self-service and gladly incur the cost of their effort; other customers find self-service too "costly." Clearly, service process designers need to recognize these trade-offs and take heterogeneous customer value judgments into account.

These two points create both challenges and opportunities for designing service processes. The challenges are understanding what trade-offs customers are willing to make and what criteria they use for evaluating the service experience. However, these challenges also create opportunities for hitting the "value sweet spot" for a customer segment based on a deeper understanding of how these customers perceive benefits and costs. But because value is co-created, we also need to explore the role the service provider plays in determining where this sweet spot is.

Value from the Service Provider's Perspective

Companies are in business to earn profits. Although this statement clearly applies to for-profit firms, even not-for-profit organizations need to have "revenues"—maybe in the form of donations or grants—that must equal or exceed their costs in order to remain viable in the long term. So, at a basic financial level, service providers derive value from selling services at prices that are greater than their costs. Many firms take a portfolio approach to this idea of "value"; for strategic reasons, management may decide to price a particular service at breakeven, or at a loss, if it contributes to an overall expected increase in profitability at the firm level. Discounts for first-time customers and coupons are a case in point. Businesses that offer discounted services through the online deal marketplace Groupon (the name is a blending of "group" and "coupon"—as each deal originally required a minimum number of people to sign up for anyone to get the deal) hopes to generate upselling and cross-selling revenues when the customer redeems the Groupon and increase their customer base to secure future profits in excess of lost revenue today.[22] But regardless of whether profitability targets are at the service product line or firm level, value to the service provider is linked to profitability.

However, profits for many Groupon merchants have been elusive. Often the deal itself is a money loser, with profitability tied to future purchases as repeat customers. If these subsequent purchases fail to materialize, any initial losses become permanent. Recognizing this, Groupon is pivoting to a strategy that emphasizes the importance of customer retention to merchant profitability:

> This year [2020] we are evolving the brand and marketing strategy to move from deal-centric to a local experiences marketplace, illustrating for consumers the breadth and depth of "Grouponable" moments and helping merchants looking to build their businesses through customer acquisition and retention campaigns. We are already a brand known for convenience, value and discovery, and we want to evolve our image to be the go-to source for amazing things to do in your backyard and beyond.[23]

Sources of Service Provider Revenues and Costs

Thinking back to the technology-enabled service innovations described earlier, service providers incur the upfront and ongoing costs of these technologies with the expectation of higher revenues, reduced operating costs, or both—that is, increased profitability. Revenues are tied to meeting customer needs, which is a source of the interdependence between the service provider and customer that leads to value co-creation. In other words, service providers design processes—often with input from customers—to offer benefits that customers want; customers realize these benefits through their participation in the service process; and service providers are rewarded through revenues generated from customers who perceive benefits in excess of their costs. This might occur through the introduction of a self-service channel that increases market share (e.g., with a wider network of ATMs than competitors), increases revenues by

---

[22]Uenlue (2019).
[23]Groupon Q4 2019 Fact Sheet (2019).

better serving existing customers (e.g., customer-specific information stored as service inventory on e-commerce sites used for targeted recommendations and to reduce customer search costs), or appeals to a new customer segment (e.g., Zipcar). And in an attempt to stay afloat during the COVID-19 pandemic, restaurants innovated to meet customer needs by selling staples, such as flour, paper towels, and toilet paper, in addition to their menu items for takeout.[24] Because restaurants and supermarkets have different supply chains, restaurants often have in-demand goods that were in short supply at supermarkets—goods that provided a much needed source of revenue for struggling restaurants.

More broadly, the building of capabilities, either embedded in technology or based on the knowledge, skills, and abilities (KSAs) of employees, enable service firms to positively impact revenue both today and in the future. For example, firms invest in training programs to build employee capabilities that are aligned with the needs of their customer base. Zappo's new hires, regardless of their position in the company, go through a 4-week customer training program where they are immersed in the why and how of Zappo's obsession with customer service at both strategic and operational levels.[25] By the end of the training, employees know exactly how to deliver service quality as defined by Zappo's. A workforce trained to understand and provide Zappo's type and level of customer service is a core capability for meeting its customers' needs. During the training program, Zappo's offers any employee a $2,000 bonus to quit! Why would they do that? Again, it comes back to how critical the customer service capability is to their business model. Employees who do not have the commitment and passion for Zappo's brand of customer service are encouraged to self-select out, with the remaining employees onboard and capable of providing outstanding customer service.

The decision to invest in capability-building also supports the longer term strategy of the firm and revenues down the road. In 1994, FedEx started experimenting with using the Internet to strengthen its time-based business model.[26] Willing to take the chance that the Internet would never take off (imagine that!), FedEx focused on developing new

---

[24]Domonoske (2020).
[25]Hsieh (2010).
[26]Hayes and Upton (1998).

operating capabilities and a competitive advantage to drive future revenues and growth. Obviously, this worked out well for FedEx. However, at the time it was a risky bet with known costs but uncertain revenue-side implications, making it difficult to actually quantify the value of building Internet capabilities. This raises an important question of how to measure value, which we will come back to later in the chapter.

On the cost side of the profitability equation, cost reductions are another way to increase profits. We have already seen how self-service technologies (SSTs) move tasks to the customer to reduce paid labor costs. In terms of technologies for service provider tasks and flows, automated document search and text analytics in the legal profession vastly reduce the need for expensive labor for what would otherwise be a tremendously time-consuming task. Cogito's AI and machine-learning algorithms replace the costly manual process for evaluating the subjective aspects of interactions among call center agents and customers as well as identifying opportunities to improve the customer experience. Not only are the technologies that support the creation of digital service inventory able to collect a greater volume and variety of customer data, but they eliminate the need for, and expense of, employees repeatedly gathering the same information from customers.

Nonfinancial Drivers of Value

Whereas profitability is a key contributor to the service provider's value assessment, there is more to the picture than that. Firms are made up of people whose concept of "value" extends well beyond profit. For example, helping patients is an important motivator for healthcare professionals; successful outcomes obviously benefit patients, but their caregivers benefit as well—not just financially but also emotionally and psychologically. We have seen that careful service process design can support both helping and profitability objectives. The DMS system that has eliminated retained surgical sponges and the OR checklists that have reduced OR errors both improve clinical outcomes—helping patients—while reducing the costs of error recovery, not to mention potential lawsuits. The ability to serve a greater number of patients, for example, through the use of healthcare smart devices or telemedicine, without negative effects on the quality of care (or even with positive quality effects) can also be advantageous from both motivational and financial perspectives.[27]

Corporate social responsibility (CSR) initiatives fall into this category of value creation that is not strictly financial. CSR covers a gamut of activities related to the social and environmental impacts of business, such as sustainability, employee welfare, and community development. Although general corporate philanthropy falls under the CSR umbrella, many firms focus on efforts tied more closely to their business model. For example, Boston Medical Center is on a mission to reduce pollutants, such as fossil fuel emissions and dioxins from incinerating medical waste, that make people sick.[28] As another example, Starbucks describes their ethical sourcing program as follows:

We've always believed in buying and serving the best coffee possible. And it's our goal for all of our coffee to be grown under the highest standards of quality, using ethical trading and responsible growing practices. We think it's a better cup of coffee that also helps create a better future for farmers and a more stable climate for the planet.[29]

This statement combines business and social objectives, as well as the idea that through "doing well by doing good,"[30] CSR can contribute to profitability. Especially when CSR takes the form of the sustainability practices of "reduce, reuse, recycle," cost savings translate to the financial bottom line. However, as with "helping patients," CSR can serve as a source of employee satisfaction (and an indicator of quality for customers) above-and-beyond the direct profitability effects.

The technology-enabled service innovations that are transforming how services are delivered are now supporting CSR initiatives as well. Farmer Connect, an organization focused on enhancing transparency and sustainability in agricultural supply chains, partnered with IBM to

---

[27]Gaskill (2015).

[28]Leiber (2020).

[29]Starbucks (2020).

[30]Waddock and Smith (2000).

introduce an app that tracks coffee beans from the field to the consumer.[31] The app runs on IBM's blockchain-based platform that maintains a permanent record of every transaction in the coffee bean's journey; consumers can access this information by scanning a QR code on their purchased coffee. The ability to verify sustainable farming practices benefits both customers who prefer to do business with sustainable companies and, of course, the companies themselves.

In addition to benefits that are not easily quantifiable in terms of dollars and cents, technology and organizational changes can be disruptive to the people involved. This exacts costs on the organization in terms of lost productivity, failure to embrace (or even sabotage) the changes, and hits to employee morale. Some of these costs are clearly quantifiable, but others are more intangible. We return to the example of Cogito and the questions about its actual impact on employee performance. Anecdotes include gaming the system by saying "sorry" frequently—to indicate greater empathy on a customer call—regardless of whether the situation called for an apology. In other robot or AI-paced work environments such as warehouse order fulfillment, injuries are more common and employee stress levels are elevated, leading to burnout and high turnover.[32] These organizational costs are clearly significant—although often difficult to quantify—and show the importance of attention to and management of the people side of technology and organizational changes.

Combining the Perspectives to Co-Create Value

If "value" from the firm's perspective is closely tied to profitability, is there a framework that translates service process design to profitability? And how would value from the customer's perspective be incorporated in the framework? In other words, going back to the question we asked at the beginning of the chapter: How does the service process design bring service providers and customers together to co-create value? We are now at the point where we can answer these questions.

---

[31]Faridi (2020).
[32]Dzieza (2020).

The Service–Profit Chain

The Service–Profit Chain, first introduced in a 1994 *Harvard Business Review* (HBR) article, is a framework for linking the service delivery system to customer satisfaction, customer loyalty, and ultimately revenue growth and profitability.[33] Because of the continued relevance and influence of the framework since its original publication, HBR designated the article as a "Best of HBR" and republished it in 2008.[34] The idea is that the path to growth and profitability in service businesses starts with the design and management of the service delivery system. What the authors term "internal service quality" is the foundation for the Service–Profit Chain reaction. Internal service quality includes elements such as work environment and job design; employee selection, development, rewards, and recognition; and tools for serving customers that give employees the ability, authority, and motivation to deliver results to customers. If internal service quality is high, employees not only have the training and resources to meet customer needs but also receive other tangible and intangible benefits (e.g., the gratification from helping people or working for a socially responsible firm). This leads to employee satisfaction, which in turn reduces turnover and increases employee productivity. More recently, these desirable employee outcomes have been aggregated as "employee engagement," with a scorecard to measure levels of employee satisfaction, identification, commitment, loyalty, and performance.[35] Interestingly, our world of ubiquitous customer feedback (e.g., surveys, online reviews) on employee performance—which can be "highly subjective, emotionally charged, and potentially biased"—has only reinforced the importance of internal service quality.[36] Frontline employees need to know that the "company has their back," providing clarity on reasonable versus unreasonable customer requests and behavior and prioritizing employee well-being—thereby, creating a positive work environment and robust tools for meeting customer needs.

---

[33]Heskett et al. (1994).
[34]Heskett et al. (2008).
[35]Kumar and Pansari (2015).
[36]Merlo et al. (2019).

Loyal employees who stay with the service firm have a positive impact on the Service–Profit Chain for three reasons. First, these employees have built customer relationships over time—and the recurring revenues that go along with them—that new employees lack. Second, experienced employees have come down the learning curve and know how to meet customer needs efficiently and effectively. Third, recruiting, hiring, and training new employees are expensive. So not only are loyal employees more productive but the firm also avoids the costs of high employee turnover.

However, employee productivity means more than just the ratio of output quantity to input costs or labor hours. We also need to take into account performance on other dimensions that customers value—quality, delivery, flexibility, innovation—and that support the firm's market position. If performance is high on the dimensions that the target market cares about, this drives customer service value while further reinforcing employee loyalty. The value the customer receives from the service leads to customer satisfaction and customer loyalty. Finally, satisfied and loyal customers drive revenue growth and profitability. This is the essence of the Service–Profit Chain. Since it was first proposed almost 30 years ago, the Service–Profit Chain has been tested in many different service contexts, with consistent support for the relationships in the framework.[37]

Let's look at an example of the Service–Profit Chain in action. The Ritz-Carlton's motto is, "We are ladies and gentlemen serving ladies and gentlemen." This is the overarching principle that sets the stage for its "Gold Standards," the values by which the brand operates.[38] The Gold Standards touch on all aspects of internal service quality for superior employee value that drives unparalleled customer service. For example, every employee completes at least 250 hours of training each year—well in excess of other hotel chains. In addition, employee empowerment is a key value. Every employee, from housekeeping to management, can spend up to $2,000 *per guest, per day* to resolve a problem without seeking permission for a supervisor. Employees are entrusted with decision-making authority to do what is best for customers—including proactively identifying and fulfilling their unexpressed needs—which drives employee

---

[37]Briggs, Deretti, and Kato (2020); Hogreve, Iseke, and Derfuss (2017).
[38]Morin (2019).

satisfaction, loyalty, performance, and customer value. This unrelenting focus on customer value keeps the Ritz-Carlton at the top of J.D. Power's North America Hotel Guest Satisfaction Index,[39] with revenue per available room, a metric used in the hospitality industry to measure hotel performance, the highest of all Marriott International brands.[40]

Value Co-Creation Framework

But completing the picture of how value co-creation results from this chain of events requires us to more explicitly include the cost side of the value equation. Although the Service–Profit Chain focuses on the positive revenue effects on profitability, we know that these revenues come with costs for the service firm, in the form of resources and capabilities. These resources (human, capital, information) and capabilities (defined as the ability to configure and use resources to create stakeholder value) are the basis for the internal service quality elements discussed above and in the Ritz-Carlton example. However, they can also affect customer service value directly, for example, through customer interactions with self-service technologies, platforms in peer-to-peer services, and smart technologies. Thus, Figure 3.1 shows a modified framework that views the steps of the Service–Profit Chain from a value co-creation perspective. In the framework, we show value being realized at three different points, two of which are different facets of the service provider's perspective. Employee service value is determined by comparing the benefits of internal service quality to the time and effort required to perform the job. For customer service value, we described earlier how the benefits revolve around meeting customer needs and that value is assessed relative to the price of the service and the customers' own time and effort as co-producers. Profitability is an indicator of value co-creation at the firm level that reflects both short-term results and the long-term effects of investing in capabilities and other revenue-producing initiatives. The steps in the Service–Profit Chain drive the revenue side of the profitability equation through customer satisfaction and customer loyalty. But the firm also incurs costs—resources and capabilities—to generate these revenues, which

---

[39]Kickham (2018).
[40]Marriott International 2019 Annual Report.

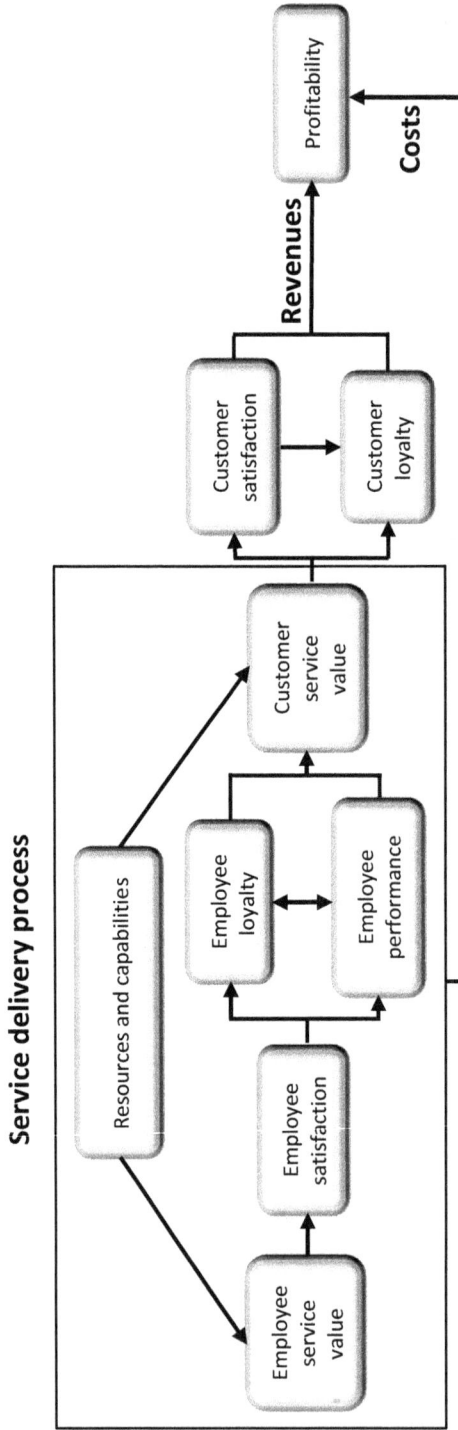

Figure 3.1 Value co-creation framework

Source: Adapted in part from Heskett et al. (2008).

is indicated in the arrow from the service delivery process to profitability in the value co-creation framework in Figure 3.1. The net value for each party is then the difference between their benefits and costs that, taken together, determines the overall value co-created in the service process.

Figure 3.1 helps answer the questions we posed earlier. It shows how the service process design brings service providers (employees and the firm) and customers together to co-create value and the series of steps by which this happens. But if we look more closely, we can draw out specific insights into the interdependencies among the three different value perspectives. As a result, we can move toward a more systematic procedure for unlocking value co-creation that takes into account the benefit and cost trade-offs and synergies for all participants in the service process in order to optimize overall realized value.

What are these insights? First, the service provider value perspective really consists of two different perspectives—that of the employees and that of the firm. Of course, the employees' interests are tied to the success of the firm; in that sense the two value perspectives overlap. However, while internal service quality directly increases employee service value, putting the internal service quality system in place is, on the other hand, a cost for the firm. But based on Figure 3.1, these firm-level costs should also be viewed as investments in human capital that ultimately benefit the firm through higher revenues. Understanding this gives us a method for evaluating how internal service quality costs impact value throughout the service process from employees to customers to the firm. It also focuses potential internal service quality investment decisions first on how they contribute to the employees' value perspective and then on the linkages to profitability.

Second, employees, customers, and the firm all receive benefits and incur costs in the value co-creation process, but a cost may be incurred elsewhere in the process than where a benefit is received. We just saw this in the case of internal service quality benefits for employees that are paid for by the firm. Although this may seem fairly obvious—after all, Figure 3.1 shows resource and capability costs at the firm level that support both employee and customer value—this type of cost and benefit pairing can be missed. SSTs are a good example. Firms benefit from reductions in paid labor costs but customer time and effort costs increase. This is the obvious part of the cost and benefit pairing. The not-so-obvious part is that self-service fundamentally changes the customer experience, which can lead to unexpected costs for the customer (e.g., feelings of frustration when attempting to navigate an interactive voice response [IVR] system) that need to be added to the value calculations.

Third, and most importantly, the tight coupling of service provider and customer value suggests that all benefits and costs throughout the process should be evaluated for synergies and trade-offs. Take, for example, the relationship between capacity costs and customer waiting times. Retailers that add more servers (salespeople, cashiers, checkout lanes, operating hours) reduce customer waiting time by trading off a cost (added capacity) to the firm with a benefit (less waiting) to the customer. This is a trade-off the Massachusetts RMV made when increasing their operating hours at their busiest branch locations—that is, adding more capacity in an existing delivery channel. But the RMV also added capacity through a new online channel. Clearly, the RMV incurred upfront costs for developing the website and have ongoing costs for maintaining and improving it. However, compared to in-person transactions at a branch, an online channel typically has much lower variable costs. In banking, another transactional service, the internal activity-based costing studies of the level and cost of resources to support transactions in different banking channels of a large U.S. bank found that, when the normalized cost of a bank branch transaction is set to $1, the cost of an online transaction is $0.09.[41] As more customers shift to the online channel, the RMV can decrease branch capacity—and its costs—while still reducing the waiting time for customers who visit a branch. As a result, the introduction of an online delivery channel eventually achieves both overall cost savings and shorter customer waits. In other words, it leads to process synergies.

Earlier we asked the question about why the RMV should care about reducing customer waiting times and improving the customer experience. After all, it is a monopoly for the services it provides. One answer is that by adding an online channel, the RMV benefits from lower transaction costs—which just so happens to reduce customer waiting times as well. However, that does not explain why the RMV would be willing to add

---

[41]Campbell and Frei (2010).

expensive capacity at its branches. This is where employee service value and its link to customer service value come into play. What managers at the RMV seem to have realized is that long customer waits have a negative impact on employee service value as interactions with dissatisfied (and often angry) customers can create an adverse work environment. This, in turn, further eroded customer service value and contributed to the negative reputation of the RMV. As customers became more vocal in their dissatisfaction with the existing service model, these costs to the RMV were amplified. Thus, the changes in the service process that focused on improving the customer experience had a broader effect that led to increased value not only for customers but also for employees and the RMV.

Because of the benefit and cost trade-offs and synergies among employees, customers, and the firm, service process design decisions must be evaluated within a holistic framework of net value co-creation across the service process participants. Understanding how these benefits and costs interact is critical to designing service processes that combine the perspectives of the customer and service provider to enhance value. Depending on the type of service (e.g., transactional versus customer-intensive), the nature of the benefit and cost interactions can vary (Box 3.3).

Box 3.3

Value co-creation in customer-intensive services

In a very different context from the fast-food drive-thru industry we considered in Box 3.2, another study[42] considers how customers trade-off quality (a benefit) with waiting times and price (costs) in customer-intensive services. These types of services involve significant interpersonal interaction between the customer and service provider. Examples include health care, legal and financial consulting, and personal care (e.g., hair salons). For customer-intensive services, customers (and often service providers) perceive an association between service speed and quality; the faster the service delivery—that is, a

---

[42]Anand, Pac, and Veeraraghavan (2011).

shorter amount of time with the service provider—the lower the perceived quality. Pressures on primary-care physicians to see more patients for shorter visits exemplifies this conundrum—many patients and physicians feel quality suffers with reduced face time. However, longer visits result in lengthier waits. So taking quality, waiting times, and price into account, customers use the service only if their net value calculation is positive. Because of the trade-off between quality and speed, the only way for quality to go up without adding to waiting times is for the number of competing service providers in a market to increase. This growth in capacity enables each service provider to spend more time with customers (a benefit). Any increase in the price of the service can then be justified by the greater benefit to the customer. When the customer benefit (time with the service provider) is exactly offset by an increase in a customer cost (price of the service), the customer's overall value calculation is unchanged. This leads to an interesting conclusion; more competition in customer-intensive services results in *higher*, not lower, prices—but only to the extent that customers value the additional time with the service provider. As a result, service provider value increases (higher prices) with no change in customer value (more time with the service provider offset by the increased price) for a net increase in service process value.

Incorporating the Three Trends into the Value Co-Creation Framework

The Rapid Pace of Technology-Enabled Service Innovation and Expanded Role of the Customer

In the previous chapter, we identified the rapid pace of technology-enabled service innovation, the expanded role of the customer, and the increasing use of service inventory as three important trends in service process design that influence value co-creation. Many of the examples in this chapter have highlighted the impact of new technologies through examples of how these technologies are driving faster delivery, higher quality, greater flexibility, and more innovative services that better meet existing and new customer needs—quite often at a lower cost. But to realize the overall value co-creation potential of technology-enabled service innovations, it is critical to consider how the technologies are experienced by participants in the service process and understand the associated benefits and costs. Otherwise, service process designers will miss opportunities to modify the process design to reinforce the benefits and mitigate the costs. The hasty move to online and distance learning during the COVID-19 pandemic precluded a detailed consideration of how to optimize the service process design and, not surprisingly, initial solutions required adjustments as unanticipated costs emerged. For example, K-12 education initially designed for synchronous delivery during the usual school day has been difficult to manage for working parents with young children. As a result, many school districts have moved to a more flexible homework schedule and asynchronous content that can be completed on weekends. In addition, instructors have had to scale back on or redesign course content because of latencies in technologies eating into class time (e.g., going into and out of Zoom breakout rooms). As educators, students, and technology providers gain more experience with online and distance learning approaches, expect to see changes in the technology itself and instructional processes to reduce these and other frictions while improving the educational experience and outcomes.

In a twist on balancing benefits and costs through technology, some companies are using AI to determine customer service breaking points.[43] For example, how long will a customer wait to get through to a human customer service agent before hanging up? How many attempts will customers make to resolve a problem before switching to another provider? Rather than trying to mitigate costs, this approach seeks to maintain customer loyalty at a minimum cost. From the customers' perspective, their time and effort costs go up, but—if "calibrated" accurately by the software—not enough to leave the current provider. Arguably, each party sees benefits in excess of costs (although just barely by the customer)—an outcome we have been promoting in this book. Although this may be true in the short term, the customer bad will engendered by this approach likely tips the value co-creation scale toward the negative side in the long term.

With more service tasks being performed by customers through SSTs, designing and managing the interface between the technology and customer become key drivers of value co-creation. From the service provider's

---

[43]Terlep (2019).

perspective, the impetus for introducing self-service is often cost reduction. But to achieve this, customers must be willing and able to move to
the self-service channel and away from higher cost delivery channels. This
gets back to the importance of understanding how customers experience
SSTs and designing the service process with all aspects of customer service value in mind. The patient check-in kiosks produced by Connected
Technology Solutions (see Box 2.1) are easy to use, secure, and accessible
to all patients, including those in wheelchairs. By explicitly designing the
kiosks based on features that are important to patients, they become an
attractive check-in option, resulting in adoption rates much higher than
expected, and therefore a substantial cost saving for healthcare providers.

The Increasing Use of Service Inventory

How does service inventory fit in the value co-creation framework
in Figure 3.1? Faster service delivery and, in the case of building
customer-specific service inventory, a more individualized service experience increase customer service value. But service inventory is also a tool
employees can use to deliver results to customers. Service inventory in the
form of remote monitoring databases allow technicians to anticipate and
quickly solve problems. Customer information stored as service inventory
in call center support systems enables employees to provide better service
with less effort, improving both employee and customer service value.
Of course, the firm pays to develop and maintain digital service inventory systems. However, once the system is in place, the marginal cost of a
unit of service inventory is low, so the benefit of service inventory to the
firm increases as demand goes up due to lower average unit costs through
economies of scale. Moving from undifferentiated provider-created to
customer-specific co-created service inventory adds further value to the
process. Each time a customer uses a service is an opportunity for the service provider to gather more customer information and further tailor the
service inventory. Service inventory more closely aligned with individual
customers increases customer service value and, according to the value
co-creation framework, leads to customer satisfaction, customer loyalty,
and higher revenues.

Service process designers can also use the value co-creation framework
to position service inventory in the service process. Firms contemplating

moving from the use of undifferentiated to customer-specific service inventory need to consider both the costs of collecting the information and the amount of additional service provider effort required—and then evaluate these costs relative to the benefits to the service process participants. This explains why Radian only acquires and stores undifferentiated service inventory; completing the title insurance process for individual customers before demand involves a significant amount of time and effort for each title and, unlike the collection of property records, no economies of scale. The cost would be prohibitive and the likelihood of any particular unit of service inventory being used is miniscule. Clearly, the overall value of positioning service inventory any closer to the customer is negative as any customer benefit of even faster delivery would be dwarfed by the costs to Radian.

Contrast this with Apple Maps that generates individualized customer travel suggestions based on the information gathered from customer usage. Because the process of formulating travel recommendations is automated, pushing individualized service inventory to the customer in a proactive process increases customer service value with little incremental cost to create it. But while we are on the subject of benefits and costs for proactive services, some customers consider unwanted service inventory pushed to them as an annoyance "cost" (Stop telling me what you think I want to purchase online!) that must be factored into the value equation.

In Figure 2.2, we showed how the level of customer involvement in creating service inventory and the degree of service inventory differentiation are matched to three different types of service inventory. We labeled two undesirable positions on the figure as "Data not available" and "Data not exploited." Both positions limit the firm's ability to create customer-specific service inventory—but for different reasons. "Data not available" is due to limited involvement with the customer. This may be a process design decision by the firm, but it could also reflect the costs customers place on providing their information. Even if the service provider has a system in place to capture customer information, customers can influence their level of involvement with the service provider and information released by choosing whether to provide their personal information and allow their usage behavior to be tracked (with loyalty cards, for example). Customers are heterogeneous in this regard; based on the costs they ascribe to their time, effort, and privacy, customers may or may not want to put in the effort to enter personal information and may or may not be willing to share this information.[44] In 2016, the General Data Protection Regulation in the European Union made data privacy a customer right by giving customers more control over their personal data and whether and how it is acquired and used. Thus, if the firm considers the creation of customer-specific service inventory as value-creating and a potential competitive advantage, the service process must be designed to reduce customers' perceived costs by alleviating customer concerns (e.g., with secure websites and limited information use guarantees) or incentivizing customers to provide information (e.g., home services using smart thermometers and smart lighting fixtures can be delivered proactively with more customer-specific information[45]).

Why might we see firms in the "Data not exploited" position in the lower right corner of Figure 2.2? A high level of customer involvement, either interpersonally or through SSTs, means customer data are available but were either not collected or not used to create customer-specific service inventory. Again, this could be a choice by the firm not to invest in the data-capture technologies and processes. But as the costs of data-capture technologies decrease and the processes for collecting a greater volume and variety of Big Data about customers improve, fewer firms are opting out of gathering customer data altogether. Call centers have been at the forefront of designing information systems to construct and benefit from customer-specific service inventory. Typically on a smaller scale, restaurateurs are now incorporating service inventory into their processes by adopting restaurant management systems such as Open Table to collect and store information on customer preferences, allergies, special occasions, and so forth, in order to personalize the service experience. However, even today, many firms struggle to make sense of so much Big Data coming at them so quickly, unintentionally leaving these firms in the "Data not Exploited" position. As an executive in the telecommunications industry stated, "With smartphones reaching billions and IoT tiptoeing into everyday appliances, the challenge has moved from data scarcity to data abundance. The winner will be whoever can handle a torrent of unstructured and structured data and convert those data into

---

[44]Li et al. (2020).
[45]Bray (2020b).

actionable information."[46] The healthcare industry is a noteworthy example of the challenges service providers face when trying to move from this position—the industry continues to grapple with converting Big Data from patients into meaningful information, including linking any insights from the data to electronic medical records.[47]

Although the "Data not Available" position is shrinking as more firms are collecting information from customers through their interactions with products and services, this trend highlights the importance of carefully considering whether or how that data will be exploited. The example of services provided through IoT devices is instructive in this regard. On one hand, proactive services using IoT devices—where the expressed purpose of creating service inventory is to identify service needs and deliver services proactively without human intervention—are often faster, better, and cheaper. On the other hand, value co-creation may be impacted in unexpected (and not always beneficial) ways. For example, connected cars collect operational data, as customers expect, but some also record more personal information such as front-seat passenger's weight.[48] In addition, the connected car IoT network can easily be expanded to include external partners such as Google or Apple. As Ford's executive director for connected vehicles and services stated, "We want to make sure our customers have a chance to give informed consent [on how details about their habits are used]." In other words, "the connected car will be a wonderful convenience or an intrusive nightmare, depending on your tolerance."

Summary: Viewing Service Process Design Through a Value-Based Lens

These examples illustrate that when designing service processes—particularly ones that incorporate new technologies, involve the customer as co-producer, and use service inventory—the full range of benefits and costs may not be immediately apparent. This is especially true when considering innovative services, such as "super-services" where the benefits and costs may not be as well established. But identifying a more complete

---

[46]Mehta (2019).
[47]Topol (2015).
[48]This example is based on Welch (2016).

set of benefits and costs is a necessary first step for accurately gauging value co-creation. This requires working toward a better understanding of how the customer and service provider (at both the employee and firm levels) perceive value, how these perspectives are related through the value co-creation framework, and how to recognize and manage synergies and trade-offs throughout the service delivery process. Although this generally summarizes the value-based approach to service process design, later in the chapter we will propose a more formal procedure.

So far, we have been focusing on "value" primarily at a conceptual level. There is a good reason for this. Before attempting to quantify "value," we needed a solid foundation for identifying the set of underlying benefits and costs to be quantified. That is why we first introduced the value co-creation framework, provided examples of its use, and considered how technology-enabled service innovations, the expanded role of the customer, and the use of service inventory could be incorporated in the framework. With the fundamentals in place, we can now move on to the question of how we can actually measure value co-creation.

Measuring Value Co-Creation

Quantifying the economic value of any service process investment is difficult because the benefits and costs are both tangible and—this is the difficult part—intangible. Tangible benefits and costs are straightforward to measure in terms of their financial impact and tend to be the basis for calculations of economic value using standard tools such as a simple return on investment (ROI) or net present value (NPV). For a law firm deciding whether to use text analytics services for document scanning, indexing, and search, the ROI or NPV calculations would include the cost of the service and the savings in manpower expenses from the reduction in manual efforts. A positive ROI or NPV supports moving to text analytics services because the in-house labor savings exceed the cost of the service over a particular time period (ROI) or on a discounted case flow basis (NPV).

Measuring Intangible Benefits and Costs

But what about "intangible" benefits or costs? What are the challenges in quantifying their economic value? Intangible benefits and costs are characterized by uncertainty in the forecast of their financial effects and an indirect relationship between the operational benefit and its economic impact.[49] In the case of text analytics services, improvements in the quality of the outcomes (e.g., more relevant information extracted from the documents and lower error rates when cataloging the information) and in the workplace and job design (e.g., a less tedious document search process for employees) are all benefits that share these characteristics. As a result, they are more difficult to financially quantify than direct labor cost savings.

Arguments have been made on both sides of the question of whether intangible benefits and costs can (or should) be financially quantified.[50] On one hand, because measurement of the economic impact is often subjective (e.g., how can "a less tedious process" be measured?) with an indirect link to financial outcomes, some people suggest dividing the analysis into quantitative and qualitative components. A "qualitative ROI" includes the intangible benefits and costs directly, without converting them to dollars and cents. As a result, the qualitative ROI necessarily involves judgments about the weights to assign each benefit and cost. These weights reflect the importance of a particular benefit or cost for meeting customer needs and co-creating value. All else being equal, an investment with a positive effect on an important (highly weighted) benefit would have a larger qualitative ROI than if the benefit had a lower weight. Alternatively, a text analytics service with better quality outcomes and a less tedious process would have a larger qualitative ROI than a similarly priced service that was inferior on these dimensions. Both the quantitative analysis based on tangible benefits and costs as well as the qualitative analysis would then be considered when designing the service process.

The "Return on Quality" Approach

On the other hand, the value co-creation framework gives us a way to at least think about financially quantifying value—even if some of the benefits and costs are intangible—through the linkages between resources and capabilities, employee service value, customer service value, and

---

[49]Glomark-Governan (2006).
[50]Gantry Group (2002).

profitability. Using a very similar framework, researchers have developed a metric termed "return on quality" (ROQ) to evaluate the financial return on service quality investments.[51] The idea is that improvements in service quality both positively impact quality perceptions and often reduce costs. High quality perceptions lead to satisfied and loyal customers who help attract new customers through word of mouth. As a result, revenues, market share, and profitability increase. And if the increase in profitability exceeds the investment in service quality (a positive ROQ), service process value goes up. From this description, one should recognize that an investment in service quality is really an investment in the service delivery process to enhance employee and customer service value as in Figure 3.1. So ROQ is more generally a measure of service process value co-creation.

The ROQ procedure starts by identifying candidate service quality improvement opportunities based on customer surveys, market information, internal information, and managerial judgment. As customer satisfaction is the linchpin in the chain of events that impacts the revenue side of the profitability equation, prioritization of these opportunities should focus on the likely effect on customer satisfaction. Using the information collected in the first step, the ROQ is estimated and the most promising opportunities chosen. At this point, estimates of revenue and market share effects—and perhaps of costs and cost-reduction potential—are still highly speculative. The next step is to implement these opportunities on a limited basis to gather hard data to make more accurate estimates of their effectiveness. Full rollouts of opportunities that continue to show promise then provide the data to calculate the final ROQ.

An example illustrates how this procedure can generate the hard numbers needed for the ROQ calculation.[52] On the basis of the responses to a customer survey, a large national hotel chain determined that satisfaction with the bathroom had the largest impact on overall customer satisfaction and that cleanliness of the bathroom was the most important predictor of satisfaction. Management decided to vary the amount of time the cleaning staff spent on bathrooms at a set of test hotels. The resulting data showed that customer satisfaction increased rapidly with additional cleaning time

---

[51]Rust, Zahorik, and Keiningham (1995).

[52]The reader is referred to Rust et al. (1995) for a more detailed description of this example and procedure for calculating return on quality.

and then leveled off. Using the original survey data to estimate the effect of increased customer satisfaction on repurchase intentions and profitability, the maximum NPV occurred with an increased cleaning staff cost equivalent to spending about two and half times as long on bathrooms. With a 3-year timeframe and a 15 percent discount rate, the calculated ROQ was 44 percent. So using customer and process data and the relationships in a value co-creation framework, "cleaner bathrooms," which would usually be considered an intangible benefit, was monetized and the investment turned out to generate a very healthy return.

But can the ROQ procedure be scaled up to evaluate new service process designs or more extensive changes in an existing process design—with multiple benefits and costs, synergies, and trade-offs? In theory, yes. But as the previous example demonstrates, even a relatively straightforward service process improvement initiative involves substantial data collection efforts and several steps to convert operational metrics (bathroom cleanliness) to profitability through the estimated effects on and financial quantification of customer satisfaction and loyalty.

The "Balanced Scorecard" Approach

So where does this leave us in terms of measuring service process value co-creation that combines the perspectives of the customer and service provider? And how do we factor in strategic issues related to the competitive environment and positioning of a particular service process within the firm's portfolio of service processes? Considering the difficulties of financially quantifying every benefit and cost, is it possible to measure overall service process value co-creation in a way that is credible to decision makers? To answer these questions, we look to an approach—the balanced scorecard—that has proven successful for understanding and managing business performance at the firm level. The motivation for developing the balanced scorecard was the realization that traditional financial measures are not sufficient to manage effectively.[53] Managers also need direct visibility into the activities and processes that drive financial results—both today and in the future. To provide a more complete set

---

[53]The description of the balanced scorecard is based on Kaplan and Norton (2005); Kaplan and Norton (2007).

of measures to guide managerial decision making, the balanced score-card includes four perspectives: one for financial goals and measures and three others for operational goals and measures focused on the customer, internal processes, and innovation and learning activities. The key perfor-mance indicators (KPIs) in the balanced scorecard reflect the firm's com-petitive priorities and the performance measures that are most important for meeting its goals.

These perspectives should look familiar. The financial goals and measures (termed the "financial perspective" in the balanced scorecard) are a lot like firm service value (profitability) in the value co-creation framework. There are similar connections between the balanced score-card customer and internal process perspectives and customer and em-ployee service value, respectively. In addition, the innovation and learning perspective is focused on capability-building that supports the current and future firm strategy and drives value to the other three perspectives. Figure 3.2 shows the mapping of the balanced scorecard perspectives to

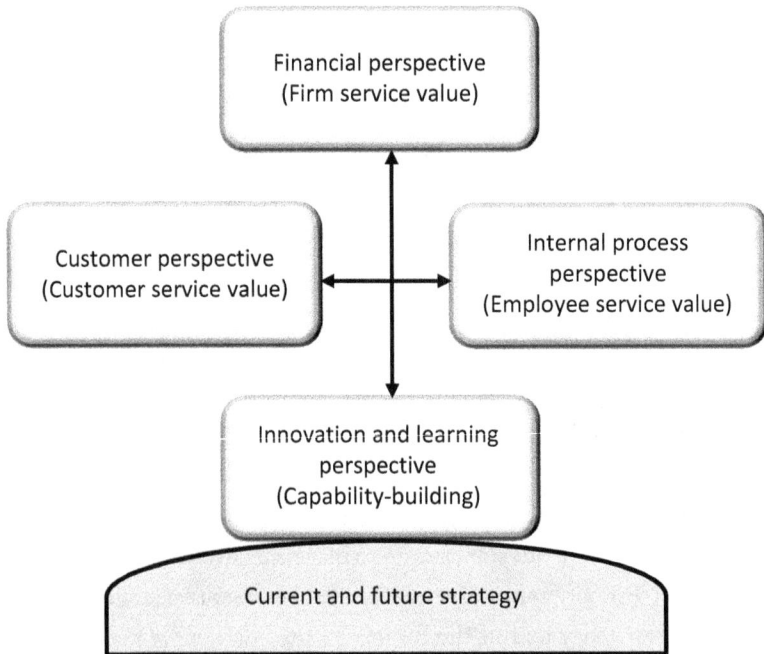

Figure 3.2 Mapping the balanced scorecard perspectives to the value co-creation framework

Source: Adapted from Kaplan and Norton (2005).

the value co-creation framework. Of course, because these perspectives are interdependent, changes in one can and will affect the structure of the others as is indicated by the double-headed arrows.

The balanced scorecard approach provides other useful insights that can be applied to measuring value co-creation at the service process level. It forces managers to identify a comprehensive set of performance measures from four different perspectives and carefully consider potential synergies and trade-offs. In fact, companies have used the balanced scorecard not only to track performance but also to validate the relationships among the measures and guide performance improvement efforts.

The Value Co-Creation Measurement Model

The value co-creation measurement model in Table 3.1 shows how both the service provider and customer benefits and costs identified earlier are connected to a measurement approach based on the balanced scorecard. All benefits and costs—both tangible and intangible—are measurable in some way, including perceptions of the customer's experience or the employee's job design and work environment. The measures shown in Table 3.1 are for illustrative purposes only; the appropriate measures for any firm or process will vary. Using the value co-creation framework in Figure 3.1 to specify relationships (synergies and trade-offs) among the measures, service process design options can be evaluated through, for example, a combination of quantitative and qualitative ROI or by converting these measures to financial outcomes to calculate ROQ. Of course, designing a service process involves multiple iterations as designers consider different options, adjust designs to enhance benefits, reduce costs, reinforce synergies, mitigate trade-offs, and gather data to more objectively and accurately determine benefits, costs, and their cause-and-effect relationships. As with the balanced scorecard, managers can track process performance using the value co-creation measurement model to continually reassess and improve the service process design. This allows service process designers to take a long-term strategic view to changing or improving the service process design over time and as business conditions change. But keep in mind that without the type of systematic approach to defining the benefits, costs, and relationships laid out here, none of this would be possible.

Table 3.1 Value Co-Creation measurement model

Firm service value		Customer service value	
Benefits	**Measures**	**Benefits**	**Measures**
Revenue	Sales and sales growth, market share, repurchase intentions, market expansion	Delivery speed Quality Flexibility	Total process time Customer ratings Number of delivery channels
Cost reduction	Cost savings	Innovation	Customer adoption of new services
Costs		**Costs**	
Service delivery process	Upfront and ongoing resource costs	Price Customer time and effort	Purchase price Waiting time, self-service time, customer experience perceptions
		Benefit trade-offs	Range of services offered versus total process time

Employee service value		Capability-building	
Benefits	**Measures**	**Benefits**	**Measures**
Internal service quality	Employee perceptions of job design and work environment, training hours, level and types of resources for meeting customer needs, employee pay	Supports the firm's strategy	Perceived alignment with firm strategy, revenue contribution to the service process portfolio
		Drives current and future firm, customer, and employee service value (increases benefits or reduces costs)	Projected revenue growth and market share, level of KSAs, customer efficiency, cost savings
Costs		**Costs**	
Employee time and effort	Employee productivity, employee experience perceptions	Investment in capability-building	Upfront and ongoing costs

Going back to the supermarket, let's reconsider how the decision to add a self-service checkout channel might work using the value co-creation measurement model. As a cost-reduction initiative, the direct cost benefits accrue to the supermarket that now needs fewer cashiers. But this only works if customers actually utilize the self-service channel at a rate proportional to the added capacity. If not, either customers endure long waiting times in the full-service lines or the supermarket has to add back cashiers to reduce waits. Both scenarios negatively affect the value of self-service. Clearly then, the key to value co-creation is to design the self-service checkout process so that customers want to—or at least are indifferent to—using the self-service channel. Recall that customers take 50 percent longer in self-service than full-service checkout. Part of the reason for this is that customer co-producers are less experienced (and therefore, slower) than employee cashiers. Thus, self-service kiosk features that reduce customer time and effort are a leverage point for value co-creation. Kiosk suppliers are stepping up to the challenge with innovations such as scanners that identify items by size and shape, eliminating a time-consuming customer task. By reducing customer costs, the convenience and control benefits of self-service checkout become appealing to a broader swath of customers—resulting in a positively reinforcing cycle of value co-creation as more and more customers use the technology. Amazon Go stores take this even further by reducing customer checkout costs to zero; customers simply pick up items and AI and cameras capture the purchase and charge the customer, eliminating the checkout process altogether.[54] Of course, supermarkets have other options as well—more employee oversight of the self-service channel, an overall increase in checkout capacity, and so forth—that impact value co-creation by providing a customer benefit but incurring a service provider cost. Determining which service process design choice is best depends on the benefits, costs, measures, synergies, and trade-offs in the value co-creation measurement model specific to the different strategies and priorities of each supermarket chain.

---

[54]Grewal et al. (2020).

Summary: Designing Service Processes to Unlock Value Co-Creation

This chapter concludes with a suggested procedure for designing service processes to unlock value co-creation (Box 3.4). It starts with a focus on the customer and meeting the needs of the target market(s). Each provider must then determine how to design its service processes to best fulfill these needs and enhance overall value co-creation.

Box 3.4

Steps for designing service processes to unlock value co-creation

These steps can be used to analyze an existing service process design to identify opportunities for enhancing its value co-creation potential or to help guide value co-creation for a new service process:

Establish what customer needs a service is intended to meet based on the desired competitive position and strategic priorities for its target market. For example, Commonwealth Bank of Australia's (CBA) management realized that, for their home loan business, the customer's goal was not to get a mortgage, but to buy a house.[55] (In a preview of the rest of the steps for designing service processes to unlock value, this led to the development of a smartphone app to help customers better understand pricing in their target neighborhoods. By pointing a phone at a house of interest, the app provides price history information not only on that house and but also other houses in the area. Understanding the real customer needs resulted in an innovative service process design and a great source of mortgage leads for CBA.)

Identify candidate service process designs for meeting these customer needs. Use the value co-creation framework to structure the search for design alternatives by focusing on customer and service provider value

---

[55]Weill and Woerner (2015).

co-creation. At this point estimates of value will often rely more on judgment than hard numbers. In addition to the conventional design options, consider the use of technology-enabled service innovations and service inventory, as well as possible delivery channels ranging from self-service to full-service to super-service. Based on a preliminary assessment of value co-creation and capability-building (strategic) potential, choose the most promising alternative(s) for further consideration.

Develop a list of the benefits and costs of a proposed service process design from the four perspectives in the value co-creation measurement model—firm service value, customer service value, employee service value, and capability-building. The list will include both tangible and intangible benefits and costs. Determine appropriate measures for each benefit and cost.

Specify the relationships among the benefits and costs using the value co-creation framework by answering the following questions:

Are there synergies? For example, the introduction of an online channel for customer transactions by the Massachusetts RMV reduces both service provider costs and customer waiting times.

What are the trade-offs? The firm's costs for putting the service delivery process in place support customer and employee benefits. This trade-off exists for all service process designs. Other trade-offs are more subtle. For example, the benefits of digital service inventory are offset by a perceived cost for customers with privacy concerns.

New benefits, costs, and measures may emerge during this step as service process designers develop a deeper understanding of process relationships and areas for improvement. For example, a focus on customer costs associated with self-service supermarket checkout task difficulty was prompted by the recognition of the importance of high utilization for reducing employee labor costs.

Determine whether the service process design can be modified to enhance benefits, reduce costs, mitigate trade-offs, and reinforce synergies. For example, Trader Joe's supply chain process was designed to offer customers high-quality products but keep costs down (mitigating a trade-off). As a result of cost savings in other parts of their supply chain, they can pay higher salaries that help attract employees who provide superior service and increase customer service value as in the value co-creation framework (reinforcing a synergy).

Evaluate overall process value co-creation. Use qualitative or quantitative methods, or both, as appropriate (e.g., ROQ and quantitative and qualitative ROI). This provides a baseline for reexamining and improving the service process design to further enhance value co-creation over time and as business conditions change. It also enables comparisons to estimates of value co-creation for competing services.

Iterate through the preceding steps as additional information is collected (e.g., through a small-scale process implementation test and customer surveys) to better define benefits, costs, and their relationships and to more accurately measure value co-creation.

How does this work in practice? We present two examples of service process designs that follow the principles for unlocking value co-creation outlined in Box 3.4. The first example involves two entrepreneurs who recognized the need for a simpler, more convenient process for the millions of U.S. adults who take multiple prescription medications each day—and responded by creating a new model for pharmacy services to transform the customer experience (Box 3.5).

Box 3.5

PillPack: a new kind of pharmacy for the digital age

T.J. Parker, co-founder and CEO of PillPack,[56] is a son of a pharmacist who grew up working at his dad's drugstore. Based on his early experiences and while becoming a pharmacist himself, he concluded that the traditional retail pharmacy model was too complicated and confusing, especially for customers taking multiple medications each day. For the more than 32 million adults in the United States alone who take five or more medications each day, this makes for a frustrating customer experience with frequent trips to the pharmacy and multiple pills and

---

[56]PillPack (2020); Core77 Design Awards (2014); Hedgecock (2015); Jones (2015). PillPack was acquired by Amazon in 2018 for just under $1B.

dosing schedules to coordinate. As a result, glitches such as missed doses and double dosing are common, contributing to poor health outcomes and adding billions to U.S. healthcare costs.[57] Parker, along with his co-founder Elliot Cohen, knew they could do better by reconceptualizing the entire pharmacy process. Working with IDEO Boston as a start-up in residency, an IDEO design team helped PillPack translate customer needs for simplicity and convenience into processes designed to "redefine how consumers engage with their pharmacy" and "deliver a delightful customer experience."[58]

Here are the basics on how PillPack is delivering on these goals: PillPack aggregates all the customer's prescriptions (and any nonprescription pharmacy products ordered, such as vitamins) and packages them by date and time in individual dose packs, with a shipment arriving at the customer's door every 2 weeks. Doctors send prescriptions directly to PillPack, and PillPack proactively sends refills to customers and contacts doctors if a prescription is running out. For any customer questions, pharmacists are available 24/7 by e-mail or phone. Compared to a traditional retail pharmacy, PillPack's processes are better aligned with how customers actually take medications, making it much easier to adhere to a medication regimen. At the same time, PillPack provides personalized—and discrete—service through their call center staffed by pharmacists. A simpler, more convenient, yet personalized service—delivered at the same cost to the customer as a traditional retail pharmacy—clearly unlocks value from the customer's perspective.

But how does PillPack profitably co-create customer value? This is where clever use of technology comes in.

Patient prescriptions are fed into a robot the size of a large filing cabinet. The machine contains canisters of the 400 highest volume pills used by PillPack; a pharmacist loads more unusual prescriptions by hand. Each drug is labeled by bar code and checked by both the machine and a pharmacist.[59]

---

[57]Hedgecock (2015).
[58]Core77 Design Awards (2014).
[59]Hedgecock (2015).

By automating much of this labor-intensive process, PillPack achieves both higher quality and lower costs, which helps fund their 24/7 personalized service. A win–win for PillPack and its customers.

And the PillPack app is another value-added service that anyone, not only customers, can use to help them remember when, and even where, to take their medication. "For instance, if you grab breakfast on the run each morning, and that's when you take your vitamin D, that stop at Starbucks will prompt your reminder."[60] Of course for noncustomers using the app, there is a one-click option for transferring their medications to PillPack.

High customer service value and low operations costs translate to a profitable business (margins are estimated to be 15 to 20 percent)—and one that unlocks the value co-creation potential of a previously poorly met customer need using an innovative service process design.

The second example is a more complex service—after-sales service support for mission-critical products in the commercial airline and defense industries—with a completely new approach to contracting and service process design based on a redefinition of existing customer needs (Box 3.6).

Box 3.6

Power by the hour: performance-based contracting for after-sales support services

The first step in designing service processes focused on value co-creation is determining what customer needs the service is intended to fulfill.[61] For the after-sales support services of original equipment

---

[60]Jones (2015).

[61]The descriptions of "power by the hour" and performance-based contracting are based on "Power by the Hour" (2007); Kim, Cohen, and Netessine (2007, 2017); and Guajardo et al. (2012).

manufacturers (OEMs), customer needs have traditionally been defined in terms of maintenance and repair; customers need maintenance services for equipment purchased or leased from an OEM and
repair services for malfunctioning equipment. But OEMs of mission-
critical equipment—military and commercial aircraft, defense equipment, and critical subsystems such as jet engines and avionics—are
finding that their focus on maintenance and repair masks a more basic
customer need. Because any unexpected failures and downtime are
not only extremely costly but can also put lives in jeopardy, what their
customers *really* need is consistent and reliable use of the equipment.
As a result, there has been a fundamental rethinking of the design
of the complex after-sales support services for these products. Rather
than the fixed price (a fixed fee that covers product support services
over a specified period) or cost-plus (labor and material costs plus a
profit margin) contracts that are typical in these industries, suppliers and their customers are moving to performance-based contracts
to better meet customer needs. "The idea behind [performance-based
contracting] is quite simple: One buys the results of product use (e.g.,
value creation), not the parts or repair services required to restore or
maintain a product."[62]

Performance-based contracting (PBC), known as "power by the
hour" in the private sector and as "performance-based logistics" in
defense contracting, compensates suppliers based on the actual realized product uptime; if the equipment isn't working, the supplier isn't
paid. Rolls-Royce originally coined the term "power by the hour" to
describe its performance-based contacts for engines based on compensation for hours flown; subsequently, engine manufacturers such as
Pratt & Whitney and General Electric have implemented PBC with
commercial airlines. This contracting approach realigns the incentives
in the service supply chain and has major ramifications for the service
process design. Unlike fixed cost contracts that have few provider service performance incentives and cost-plus contracts lacking in incentives to reduce costs—and, in fact, reward higher cost providers with

---

[62]"Power by the Hour" (2007).

a larger "plus"—PBC incentivizes both high service performance and low costs. Preventative maintenance and higher quality products that fail less often, as well as faster response time and better repair quality for products that do fail, all increase product uptime for the customer and revenues for the supplier. And because customers are paying for uptime and not maintenance or repair, the provider has an incentive to deliver product support services as cost-effectively as possible. In other words, performance-based contracts provide a roadmap—including benefits, costs, synergies, and trade-offs—for designing after-sales support service processes and the entire service supply chain for value co-creation.

But how can equipment suppliers determine the specific service process and supply chain design choices that work best for them and their customers? That's where the value co-creation measurement model comes in. Because revenues are tied directly to product uptime, the value of a design option can be quantified based on the option's effect on product uptime (revenues) and cost. For example, should providers invest in building maintenance capabilities? Or product design, response time, or repair capabilities? Based on their own value calculations, different providers will make different choices.

Results to date have been encouraging. Compared with cost-plus contracts, product reliability under PBC is 25 to 40 percent higher because of more frequent scheduled maintenance and better care taken in each maintenance event.[63] And improved product reliability leads to savings in acquiring and holding spare parts.[64] Higher product uptime and lower service supply chain costs add up to increased value—all because the after-sales support service process is now designed around meeting customers' real needs.

---

[63]Guajardo et al. (2012).
[64]Kim, Cohen, and Netessine (2017).

CHAPTER 4

Knowledge-Intensive Services

In the previous chapter, the value co-creation framework and measurement model were introduced to guide service process design for *all* types of services. This chapter focuses specifically on knowledge-intensive services, a particular class of services in which the service process tasks and service product are primarily centered on information and information flows.[1] Examples include professional services such as managerial and technology consulting, health care, legal services, and education. Although it has been estimated that at least 30 percent (and growing) of the U.S. workforce is engaged in knowledge work,[2] designing the service delivery processes for knowledge-intensive services presents unique challenges for the following reasons.

First, the service delivery process is "complex, unstructured, and highly customized to meet a particular client's unique needs."[3] As such, the customer must play an active role as a co-producer of the knowledge-based service product. In fact, customers typically possess information that is not known by the service provider but is necessary to complete the service. For example, a patient needs to describe his symptoms for the doctor to make a diagnosis. In managerial consulting engagements, clients frequently work alongside consultants to develop and implement solutions. Clients have information about current work processes and often ideas for improvement that are critical to the success of the consulting project. So service performance depends, to a large extent, on how effectively

---

[1]Much of the content in this chapter is based on Xue and Field (2008).

[2]Hayes et al. (2005).

[3]Bettencourt et al. (2002).

customers perform their process tasks. These examples highlight the importance of a collaborative approach to completing the nonstandard tasks typical of knowledge-intensive services.[4] Although knowledge-intensive services may also be customer-intensive (i.e., involving significant interpersonal interaction between the customer and service provider—see Box 3.3), it is the types of service product (information and information flows) and process activities performed by the service provider *and* the customer that distinguish these services from other services.

Second, because knowledge-intensive services often require substantial and multiple information transfers from the service provider to the customer and from the customer to the service provider, information transfer is a major element of the overall service process design. But information can be "sticky," causing knowledge transfers between two parties to be difficult and costly.[5] Continuing with the example of a doctor and patient, a patient providing relevant and complete information improves the doctor's ability to make a correct diagnosis. However, patients often do not know what information is relevant (e.g., recent travel and foods eaten) or have difficulty describing their symptoms, resulting in knowledge transfers from the patient to the doctor being "sticky." Clearly, an important consideration when designing the process for gathering information from the patient is how the doctor can elicit the right information for diagnostic and treatment purposes. Similarly, information transfers from the doctor to the patient must be understandable to the patient. Especially in a healthcare context, any information stickiness can have serious consequences. "Patients often ignore their doctor's orders, because they do not truly understand them, and doctors often do not understand a patient's needs or the reasons they are not taking their medications."[6] In general, facilitating information transfers between the service provider and the customer is a significant issue for knowledge-intensive services.

Third, being complex, unstructured, and highly customized, it can be difficult to completely specify the terms of a knowledge-intensive

---

[4]Roels (2014).
[5]von Hippel (1994).
[6]Weintraub (2012).

service contract upfront. This occurs with some frequency for consulting projects. The initial stages of technical and managerial consulting engagements may reveal unanticipated challenges or even opportunities that impact the direction or scope of the project. For example, consider artificial intelligence (AI)-based performance management systems and process improvement consulting projects. The organizational disruption and pushback when implementing new technologies such as Cogito's emotional intelligence evaluation and coaching system may require the project focus to temporarily shift away from the system itself to organizational change management. On the other hand, for a particularly successful process improvement project, management may choose to introduce it more widely in the organization than originally anticipated. When a renegotiation of the contract between the service provider and customer is required to redefine the requirements of the emerging service need, the original contract is termed "incomplete."[7] Incomplete contracts introduce uncertainty into the service process design and execution, particularly in terms of what process tasks will ultimately be performed and by whom.

The strongly co-productive nature of knowledge-intensive service processes, information stickiness, and the prevalence of incomplete contracts have important implications for the service process design, especially the allocation of activities between the service provider and the customer (i.e., "who does what"). We will explore how each of these features—separately and together—impact value co-creation and offer additional process design recommendations that complement the more general approach suggested so far. But to do this, we need to first look more closely at the components of a knowledge-intensive service delivery process.

The Building Blocks of Knowledge-Intensive Service Processes

What distinguishes knowledge-intensive services from other services is that the service product is primarily information-based and the core service process activities involve the acquisition, analysis, use, and transfer of information. Although these activities take place within processes

---

[7]Hart (1995).

where the service provider and customer work together closely to co-produce the service, information stickiness often inhibits the easy flow of information between them. Thus, when defining and measuring the benefits and costs—that is, the value—of knowledge-intensive services, we need to factor in the impact that information stickiness has on co-production. The process activities and context in which they take place form the building blocks that allow us to incorporate the specific design considerations of knowledge-intensive services back into the value co-creation framework and measurement model. While knowledge-intensive services may, of course, include activities that are not predominantly about information (e.g., hospital housekeeping activities carried out as part of a healthcare process), the focus in this chapter is on developing new insights into the information-based activities that form the core of knowledge-intensive service processes.

Core Activities of Knowledge-Intensive Services: Information Processing and Transfer

Considering the important roles both the service provider and the customer play in co-creating the knowledge-intensive service product and the tight linkages between the efforts of each party, the core operational activities of knowledge-intensive services are both the information processing tasks carried out by each party and the information transfers between them. What is meant by information processing is the information-based activities performed to complete the service (e.g., research, data analysis, and documentation of results). Information transfer, in contrast, is the exchange of information from one party to the other (e.g., through e-mails, meeting, PowerPoint presentations). Typically, the service provider and customer have information that is not initially known by the other party but is necessary to perform the service. For example, accountants require documents and other financial information from clients to prepare their taxes. Similarly, instructors communicate course content and instructions necessary for students to complete assignments.

More specifically, a knowledge-intensive service process consists of four types of basic activities.

Service provider information processing: To complete service tasks, the service provider processes internal information (e.g., based on their own expertise) or information acquired from the customer or other sources. For example, a doctor diagnoses a patient's condition based on her training and experience as well as information provided by the patient and the medical literature.

Customer information processing: To complete service tasks, the customer processes information they have about themselves or their organization and information acquired from the service provider or other sources. For example, a patient manages his diabetes using continuous glucose monitors and apps that monitor diet and provide peer support.

Customer-to-service provider information transfer: The customer transfers information to the service provider.

Service provider-to-customer information transfer: The service provider transfers information to the customer.

Keep in mind that these four activities are not necessarily sequential, and some of them can take place simultaneously. In addition, a knowledge-intensive service process can include multiple rounds of interactions involving information transfer and processing by both parties either working separately or together. For instance, consider brainstorming sessions with designers and their clients to sketch out a new service or product. The process involves back-and-forth information transfers of requirements, ideas, feedback, and refinements between the clients and designers. At the same time, the outline of the new service or product design is ideally the result of collective information processing efforts as designer and client concepts converge on the final design. Figure 4.1 depicts the interrelationships among information processing and information transfer in a knowledge-intensive service process, including the potential overlap of service provider and customer information processing while collaborating. In addition to information transfers between the service provider and the customer, information can be acquired from suppliers and the environment—as well as processed by any member of the service supply chain. We will consider the service supply chain in more detail at the end of the chapter.

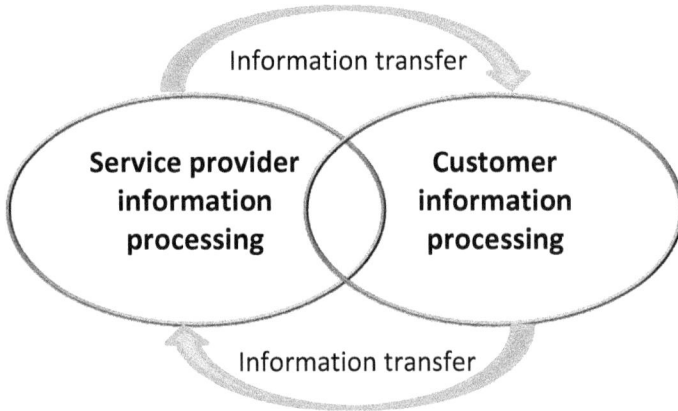

Figure 4.1 Information flows in knowledge-intensive services

For consulting and other knowledge-intensive services, information processing is usually assumed to be the primary value-adding process activity (e.g., research for and structuring of a marketing campaign strategy for a new service). Although information transfer is required for the completion of the project (e.g., the client providing background information about the new service and specifying desired goals for the campaign, communicating with regard to the implementation of the strategy), these activities are often thought to be ancillary to value co-creation.

However, for many services, the design of information transfer activities can spell the difference between success and failure in delivering on their potential value. There are at least two reasons for this. First, the overall trend toward an expanded role for the customer in service processes applies to knowledge-intensive services as well. The self-service technologies (SSTs) that patients are increasingly utilizing to monitor and even treat their own diseases require significant and, frequently, ongoing patient education—that is, information transfer—by healthcare providers if the technologies are to be correctly and consistently used. This shifting of information processing tasks to the patients—tasks that were previously done by trained providers—elevates patient education information transfers from necessary, but secondary, tasks to important value-adding activities. In addition, information about the patient's condition must be transferred back to the provider to validate the efficacy of the current treatment or indicate the need for intervention. Even though technology improvements and the introduction of smart devices that automate the information transfers (recall the example of the ProAir Digihaler for managing asthma and COPD in Chapter 2) are reducing information transfer costs—sometimes drastically—other healthcare SSTs, such as in-home self-dialysis,[8] still require considerable information transfers for patient education and monitoring.

Second, information transfer can encompass a much higher proportion of the total service work than expected. In an interview with a senior technology consultant, he estimated that the ratio between research and implementation is as low as 1:10 for projects completed by his firm. As an example, he cited one project with a budget of approximately $100,000, in which $8,000 was spent on the actual research ($3,000 for lab experiments and $5,000 for a literature review), whereas $92,000 was spent to implement the solution. To a large extent, the implementation involved information transfers—that is, meetings to explain their findings to the client and describe the steps for moving toward prototyping an actual product.

The high cost for the implementation stage often catches even experienced consultants by surprise, who expect the ratio between research and implementation to be closer to 1:1, as both they and the client view the core value of the consulting service to be created in the research stage.[9]

Easing the transfer of information from the service provider to the customer and from the customer to the service provider not only reduces the cost of these activities but, as we will see, also fundamentally alters the service design in terms of who does the information processing tasks. With fewer constraints on transferring information, information processing tasks can be done by the process participant—service provider or customer—who can perform the work most efficiently.[10] But an impediment to the free flow of information is that it is often difficult or costly to transfer from one party to another. In other words, if it is "sticky."

---

[8]National Kidney Foundation (2020).
[9]Xue and Field (2008).
[10]Roels (2014).

Information Stickiness

When we say that sticky information is "difficult" or "costly" to transfer, what exactly do we mean? A more complete definition of information stickiness provides some clarity. The stickiness of a unit of information in a particular context is "the incremental expenditure required to transfer that unit of information to a specified locus in a form usable by a given information seeker."[11] Information stickiness-related expenditures may result from delays in the communication or receipt of the information as well as explicit charges by the information provider for access to the information.[12] Thus, difficulties in information transfer arise from barriers to moving information from one party (or "locus") to another as well as whether the information—even if transferred—is usable by the recipient. These difficulties lead to higher costs for information transfer, such as additional time spent on the transfer itself (as was experienced by the senior technology consultant in his interactions with his clients) or additional information preparation to make it more understandable to the recipient (e.g., rewriting a report or PowerPoint presentation). Charging for access to information can also be considered a barrier to the flow of information from one party to another and is therefore a type of information stickiness.

These "barriers" that make information transfer difficult originate in the characteristics of the source, the recipient, the information, and the context in which it is delivered.[13] The source may simply not be a good communicator—due to either an incomplete mastery of the topic (as can happen when instructors teach outside their areas of expertise) or an inability to clearly articulate the knowledge they do have. On the flip side, the recipient may lack absorptive capacity—that is, the ability to absorb and apply information from an outside source. Most (probably, all) of us have experienced this first hand. For example, learning the basic functionality of a software program for someone who has never used it before—and certainly for someone who is unfamiliar with computers in general—typically requires a considerable amount of time and effort by

---

[11]von Hippel (1994).

[12]Ibid.

[13]The description of the sources of information stickiness is from Szulanski (2000).

the learner (and the teacher as well). This is because the recipient lacks previous knowledge and experience to build on, both specific to the software program and more broadly to computer technology. In other words, a person without any background in computers or software lacks absorptive capacity for learning a new software program. But as someone builds up a base of relevant knowledge, absorptive capacity rapidly increases. That's why learning advanced software features is often easier than learning the basics.

Both the source and recipient must be motivated to make the information transfer as smooth as possible. Of course, compensation can be an extrinsic source of motivation, for example, a bonus for early completion of a consulting project or lower costs and higher profitability when more quickly performing fixed-reimbursement services such as healthcare procedures. But the perceived reliability of the source also matters. From the recipient's perspective, reliable sources are more trustworthy, which affects their motivation to seek or accept information from that source. And a comfortable working relationship reduces the effort needed to resolve any transfer problems that may occur.

In terms of the information itself, complex or unproven knowledge increases the difficulty of the information transfer process and consequently the number of transfer iterations required. In an educational setting, complex concepts require more time to communicate and extra back-and-forth discussion between the instructor and students than simpler ideas—even if the instructor has excellent communication skills and the students have high absorptive capacity. As for unproven knowledge, speculative theories presented by litigators in the courtroom require more explanation than clear-cut arguments.

When both the need for and cost of information transfer is high—as in the case of in-home self-dialysis—investments to reduce information stickiness have the potential to greatly improve process performance. By identifying the sources of difficulties in information transfers, this provides a focus for information stickiness reduction efforts. In the next chapter, we address the question of how the capabilities of service providers and customers can be unleashed on these sources of information stickiness to improve information flows, lower service costs, and increase value co-creation. But because information transfer does not occur in isolation, we first need to understand how information transfer and information processing activities—and their costs—work in a knowledge-intensive service.

Information Transfer and Processing Costs

When designing knowledge-intensive service processes, it is important to keep in mind that both the service provider and the customers have information that is necessary for the completion of the service and that some of this information is sticky. And the greater the barriers to information transfer—from the service provider to the customer or from the customer to the service provider—the higher the information transfer cost.

In addition, the cost to process the same information can differ substantially depending on which party is doing the work. In general, the service provider is more efficient at completing the service tasks, but the customer is charged a fee—often a substantial fee—for the provider's services. This may tempt the customer to attempt self-service to "save" money. Take, for example, someone with a legal issue who can choose to either hire an attorney or represent himself. The obvious trade-off is greater efficiency of the attorney versus cost to the customer. But this should only be part of the consideration. The choice of *who* does the work affects service quality and consequently the value of the service. Due to the likely gap of skills and capabilities between inexperienced self-service customers and professionally trained service providers, any savings in attorney fees can be more than eclipsed by a poorer quality outcome. In terms of the four information processing and transfer costs, inferior service quality adds to the cost of customer information processing. So does this mean that people with legal issues should never represent themselves? The answer to this question depends on the total information processing and transfer costs and how they fit in the value co-creation framework. We will come back to this question and address it in depth in the next section on setting the task boundary between the service provider and the customer. The task boundary is a continuum that shows the proportion of the service tasks performed by the service provider versus the customer. For example, a process with a high degree of self-service moves the task boundary closer to the customer.

But before doing that, there are a few other important points to cover about the costs themselves. First, the costs must be viewed within the strategic goals of the service. For example, an enterprise resource planning (ERP) system integrates business processes across organizations using interconnected software modules. In ERP implementation consulting, the cost to transfer information from the consultant to the client is high, but "one objective for business clients is to acquire ERP-related knowledge so that they can maintain and operate the systems independent of the consultants."[14] So even if the client cannot, at least initially, process information at a lower cost than the consultant, the eventual need for independence from the consultant trumps current cost considerations. This leads to the second point. The costs and their relative magnitudes change over time. Thus, as in the case of ERP implementation, a long-term versus a short-term view can lead to very different process design decisions.

Moreover, the process design should be reevaluated over time as the information processing and transfer costs change. In the realm of consulting, subsequent engagements with the same client decrease barriers to information transfer due to the accumulation of tacit knowledge of the client's business domain and operating routines as the parties repeatedly interact.[15] We have already seen how advances in self-service medical technologies and smart devices have enabled patients to take on more monitoring and treatment tasks by reducing both their information processing and transfer costs. Although the jury is still out on online and distance learning services, the design, and implied costs, of the information transfer activities continue to be a challenge. Well-designed asynchronous online courses reflect instructor efforts to compensate for the lack of real-time instructor–student interaction and leverage the capabilities of the online delivery channel (e.g., threaded discussions and collaboration platforms). But many students still struggle with learning course material without real-time information transfer to and from a live instructor. However, as instructors and students gain experience with online and distance learning during the COVID-19 pandemic, information processing

---

[14]Ko, Kirsch, and King (2005).
[15]Ethiraj et al. (2005).

and transfer costs are decreasing. The long-term ramifications for the delivery of educational services are yet to be seen.

In summary, an accurate understanding and assessment of the four information processing and transfer costs are a precursor to designing knowledge-intensive services for value co-creation both today and over time as the costs change. The next section considers how the three challenges identified earlier—the heavy reliance on customers as co-producers of knowledge-intensive service products, sticky information that is difficult and costly to transfer, and incomplete contracts that require renegotiation as the actual service need becomes clearer—impact value co-creation. This is followed by a roadmap for designing knowledge-intensive service processes to integrate the service provider and customers, while mitigating the negative effects of information stickiness and the uncertainty of incomplete contracts. Because core activities of knowledge-intensive service processes are information processing and transfer, the focus of design decisions will be on deciding which of these tasks are to be done by the service provider, which by the customer, and where provider and customer information processing overlaps. In other words, how should the boundary between service provider and customer activities be determined?

Driving Value Through Service Process Boundary-Setting

One-Time Service Encounters

Because both the service provider and customer are co-producers of knowledge-intensive services, the determination of how to divide up the information processing tasks is a key process design decision. Our models show that, for a one-time service encounter where the service is delivered according to the initial agreement, net value is maximized when the sum of the four information processing and transfer costs is minimized. Why is this? First, when the initially agreed-upon service is unchanged over the course of the service delivery process, the final price for the service also does not vary from the initial price. Thus, with revenues held constant, any change in the service provider's profitability stems from increases or decreases in costs. Second, from the customer's perspective, any differences in the quality of the service that depend on which party performs a service task are reflected in the information processing and transfer costs, so lower quality service increases these costs. Thus, looking at value from these two perspectives, any decrease (or increase) in the net value of the service is due to higher (or lower) costs.

Returning to the question of whether self-service is a viable option for legal services, we need to compare the total information processing and transfer costs under the self-service model to the costs when going the "full-service" route and hiring an attorney. In most situations, the dramatically lower efficiency and quality of self-service is likely to result in customer information processing costs (e.g., preparing and trying the case) that are perceived to be higher than the fees charged by an attorney. Although self-service reduces information transfer costs because the customer is also the service provider, information processing accounts for the bulk of the costs for complex cases, such as criminal cases. For these types of (hopefully) one-time legal issues, the total information processing and transfer costs tend to favor hiring an attorney.

However, states such as Arizona have an online self-service center with a number of self-service forms for relatively straightforward legal tasks such as name changes and small claims.[16] The information and forms provided on the Arizona Judicial Branch website reduce the information processing costs for the customer and may tilt the total costs toward self-service. But for all self-service forms, the website offers the following disclaimer:

> The information offered on this site is made available as a public service and is not intended to take the place of legal advice. If you do not understand something, have trouble filling out any of the forms or are not sure these forms and instructions apply to your situation, see an attorney for help. Before filing documents with the court, you might consider contacting an attorney to help guard against undesired and unexpected consequences.

Even for seemingly "simple" legal tasks, this disclaimer suggests that customer information processing costs may be higher than anticipated.

---

[16]Arizona Judicial Branch (2020).

So choosing whether to use self-service or full-service requires an understanding of which option minimizes the total information processing and transfer costs, including the somewhat subjective costs of service quality.

Recurring Services

Compared with a one-time service encounter, boundary-setting becomes more complicated with recurring knowledge-intensive services. Recurring services are either the same service provider and customer pairing (e.g., long-term or repeat consulting engagements with the same client) or the same (or similar) service product for multiple customers (e.g., corporate trainers using a standard training module for different clients). In the former case, the established relationship and acquired knowledge about the customer's organization and business reduces information transfer costs from the customer to the service provider and from the service provider to the customer. In addition, service provider and customer collaborative efforts becomes more efficient and effective as the parties have more experience working with each other.

But it is not only the cost side of the equation that is affected when knowledge-intensive services are recurring; the benefits change over time as well. In the previous example of ERP consulting services, although initial information transfer costs are high, often the long-term goal is to build customer capabilities for managing the ERP system independently from the consultants. Thus, from the clients' perspective, the costs and benefits interact, with costs incurred in the short-term creating capabilities that benefit the clients—and lower their information processing costs—in the long-term. From the consultants' perspective, the pricing of their services to different clients reflects not only the changing costs over time for repeat clients but also a longer term and holistic approach to client profitability. For example, when a consulting firm charges reduced prices to attract returning business, lower service costs for repeat clients provide an additional justification for reducing prices. Again, we see that the costs and benefits interact—not only for the customer but also for the service provider. And in the case where knowledge-intensive services can be "recycled" for different customers (as with standard training modules), spreading the service provider information processing costs over multiple customers translates to greater value co-creation through a combination of reduced prices to customers and/or higher profitability to the firm.

So unlike the one-time service encounter, where process design decisions about who does what are driven by the four information processing and transfer costs, determining the service provider and customer tasks for recurring services depend on how the benefits and costs change over time. But for both one-time service encounters and recurring services, the objective is to set the task boundary to maximize value co-creation. For example, investments in building customer capabilities pay off only if customers can leverage these capabilities to fulfill subsequent service needs. For one-time service encounters, the information transfer costs to develop customer capabilities would typically far outweigh any reduction in their information processing costs and the information transfer costs. This is why self-service medical technologies, where process tasks are pushed to the patient, are primarily used for chronic conditions. In addition to lower long-term costs, patients benefit from the convenience of self-service versus repeated visits to their doctors. In fact, for management of chronic diseases such as cancer, heart disease, and diabetes, greater patient effort in general—from compliance with basic requirements to actively sharing and seeking information to connecting with others—has been shown to increase patient quality of life and satisfaction, while reducing the burden on the healthcare system.[17] However, for other types of medical conditions with single or few service encounters, value co-creation (i.e., cost minimization) generally favors boundary-setting with medical professionals performing the service process tasks.

The following example of a recurring knowledge-intensive service illustrates boundary-setting for a process with an information processing and transfer cost structure the reader may find surprising (Box 4.1).

For some knowledge-intensive services, the original service need changes over the course of the service delivery process. As a result, the initial terms of the service agreement or contract are "incomplete" and must be modified to reflect the changing service requirements. In particular, this requires a renegotiation of the workload between the service provider

---

[17]Sweeney, Danaher, and McColl-Kennedy (2015).

Box 4.1

The high costs of national security

Technologies to screen and track people and property are part of the infrastructure to secure our borders, ports, and airports. From the familiar X-ray machines at airports to fixed and mobile video surveillance systems, range finders, thermal imaging devices, radar, ground sensors, and radio frequency sensors at ports and border crossings,[18] these technologies play a key role in safeguarding national security. As a result, maintenance of this equipment is a crucial concern. Due to the critical importance of equipment uptime, remote monitoring by the equipment supplier would seem to be an ideal solution for proactively identifying maintenance needs. Because much of the technology used to secure the borders is deployed in isolated locations that are difficult and time-consuming to reach, remote monitoring has the additional benefit of potentially eliminating service technician travel time if the actual equipment maintenance can also be done remotely—or at least reduce the lead time between the proactive identification of a maintenance need and the arrival of service technicians. From an information transfer and processing perspective, this also makes sense. Using automated resources available at a remote customer support center, the equipment supplier has low information processing costs for identifying specific maintenance requirements. In addition, the electronic information transfer cost from the customer site to service provider is minimal. So in terms of overall value co-creation, remote monitoring is clearly the right service process design choice—that is, until we take into account the perceived cost of information security. If the "bad guys" have information on what and where screening and tracking equipment is down or malfunctioning, it opens up a potential opportunity to compromise national security. Because tapping into communications between the customer and service provider might provide this information, information transfer costs are, in fact, extremely high when information security costs are added to the equation. Despite the benefits of remote monitoring and lower service provider information processing costs, information transfer costs typically dominate the value calculation. Consequently, monitoring equipment and identifying maintenance needs to stay at the customer site.

---

[18]Department of Homeland Security (2018).

and customer co-producers going forward. Next, we consider how the uncertainty associated with incomplete contracts can lead to poor decisions when reallocating process tasks—and what can be done to counteract their negative impact on value co-creation.

What if the Initial Service Need Changes?

For knowledge-intensive services such as managerial and technical consulting, the service need identified at the outset may, and often does, change over the course of the consulting engagement, as the earlier examples of AI-based performance management systems and process improvement consulting projects illustrate. How, then, do these changes affect the service delivery process? Which party takes on the additional or altered tasks? Who should make that decision?

Because of the uncertainty surrounding consulting processes, contracts are commonly left incomplete, with consultants and clients renegotiating the terms of their agreement as the consulting engagement unfolds. In fact, it is common practice in consulting to include a "change management clause" in the original consulting contract, which leaves the window open for future renegotiation. These change management clauses include information on what constitutes a "change" and what steps are to be taken if there is a change. The individuals who have the authority to renegotiate the contract determine what changes have occurred or will occur and any associated adjustments in pricing and work allocation. Potential changes in the consulting engagement can be a source of tremendous conflict between the consultant and client if there is no agreement in the original contract about what will happen if changes are needed.

With an incomplete contract, if the service need turns out to be more extensive or more complicated than expected, our models show that during the renegotiation process the natural inclination is to update the contract to have the domain expert—in other words, the service provider—do additional work. After all, the service provider is typically more efficient than the customer at completing the information-based tasks. But when considering *all* service provider and customer information processing and transfer costs, this conventional wisdom is often wrong. In fact, overall value can be enhanced by pushing more of the tasks to the customer.

What accounts for this seemingly counterintuitive finding? By focusing only on *who* will complete the new tasks, information transfer costs and potential interactions among the information processing and transfer costs are not being adequately factored in. When the service provider performs more of the work, the need for information transfer from the service provider to the customer increases as well. As a result, the cost—and price—of the service provider's efforts rapidly escalates. This cost escalation intensifies when the final service need is more extensive and complicated than expected, which is exactly the situation where incomplete contracts and renegotiation are most common! Instead, if the customer can take on at least some of the tasks, the service provider's costs are reduced, as is the need for information transfer from the customer to the service provider.

Of course, any increases in the customer's information processing costs must be balanced against decreases in the other costs. But we are seeing changes in service process design—primarily technology-enabled service innovations—that allow the customer to perform information-based tasks at a lower cost.[19] For example, consultants may provide training and templates that allow clients to do more of the co-production tasks. In fact, McKinsey & Company introduced a new business line just for this purpose.[20] McKinsey Solutions works with clients to develop customized packages of databases, software, and analytical tools, and embeds them in client systems so that clients can then execute analytics tasks previously done by McKinsey.[21] And we have already described how technologies are supporting customer efforts for other knowledge-intensive services such as health care, legal, and education—where the final service need may not be known upfront—to lower their information processing costs.

But who should determine the allocation of work after the final service need is known? Whereas most change management clauses in consulting contracts stipulate that the consultant is obligated to inform the client ahead of time of anticipated changes in the engagement

---

[19]Bellos and Kavdias (2019).
[20]McKinsey & Company (2020).
[21]Groysberg et al. (2019).

(particularly, if additional consultant hours are needed), it is then the client's right to authorize the changes. However, our models show that overall value is enhanced when the consultant, rather than the client, determines who should perform the additional or altered service tasks. This is because the service provider is generally more knowledgeable about the service process task requirements and is in a better position to evaluate whether their expertise is needed for certain tasks or if a task could be done at a lower cost by the customer (e.g., using self-service McKinsey Solutions).[22] But because the customer usually has the right to determine who will do what, the reallocation of process activities can be suboptimal from a value co-creation perspective.

Summary: Recommendations for Knowledge-Intensive Service Process Design

In Box 3.4, we outlined the steps for designing service processes to unlock value co-creation. This procedure applies to any type of service process, including knowledge-intensive services. But knowledge-intensive services have some characteristics that set them apart from other services and impact how value is co-created through their service process design. In particular, knowledge-intensive services consist primarily of information and information flows. As a result, we identified the four basic activities of knowledge-intensive services as: service provider information processing, customer information processing, service provider-to-customer information transfer, and customer-to-service provider information transfer. Even though information processing is generally considered to be the core value-creating activity, information transfers impact value as well, especially if the information is difficult or costly to transfer, that is, "sticky." With service processes that tend to be complex, unstructured, and highly customized to the individual customer, knowledge-intensive service processes require close collaboration between the co-productive efforts of the service provider and the customer. Yet the actual service need may not be known upfront or may evolve over time as the service encounter progresses, so the contracts between service providers and

---

[22]Bellos and Kavadias (2019).

customers are often "incomplete." Because of the strongly co-productive nature of knowledge-intensive services, together with the potential for sticky information and incomplete contracts, the general procedure for service process design in Chapter 3 is supplemented with more specific recommendations as summarized in Box 4.2.

Box 4.2
Designing knowledge-intensive service processes

Designing knowledge-intensive service processes involves determining both *what* activities to do and *who* will do them. As a complement to the steps for designing service processes in Box 3.4, following are observations about and additional recommendations for knowledge-intensive service processes.

As information-based services, costs and benefits of knowledge-intensive services are derived from information processing and information transfer activities. Both the service provider and customer co-producers process information to complete service tasks and transfer information from one party to the other. These four activities, then, are the basis for evaluating overall process value co-creation.

For a one-time service encounter between a service provider and customer pair (e.g., a single consulting engagement or legal case) where the service is delivered according to the initial agreement, value is maximized when the sum of the service provider and customer information processing costs and information transfer costs (including any increases in costs due to poorer quality service by a less capable party) is minimized. When determining who should perform a task, the effect not only on information processing costs but also on the need for information transfers and its costs should be taken into account.

For recurring services, the benefits and costs interact as well as change over time. Information processing and transfer costs incurred early in an ongoing service provider-customer relationship can build capabilities in the long term that change the relative benefits and costs for the two parties (as in the case of an ERP consulting engagement with the long-term objective of the client firm employees operating the system independently from the consultants). Thus, the task boundaries for recurring services can either evolve as the value equation changes (e.g., customers take on more of the service tasks as their information processing costs go down) or the initial tasks are set to leverage long-term value co-creation (e.g., patients trained on and utilizing self-service medical technologies for managing chronic conditions).

If the service need changes over the course of the service delivery process and the terms of the service agreement are renegotiated, the original contract between the service provider and customer is termed "incomplete." When the final service need is known, it is important to not just automatically assign any additional or altered tasks to the service provider. Rather, consider how all four information processing and information transfer costs are affected by the changing service need. In many cases, value is increased when at least some of the new activities are allocated to the customer. Although the customer is usually entitled to determine the reallocation of work, letting the service provider, who generally knows more about the task requirements, at least weigh in on, if not determine, how the tasks are divided between the parties can positively impact value co-creation.

Because knowledge-intensive services can be customized, the task boundary for a similar service may differ depending on the service provider and customer pairing. Preferences and capabilities, and their associated benefits and costs, vary by customer, which results in value equations that are specific to the customer, even for the same service. On one extreme, if a customer is incapable of performing certain tasks and is uninterested in developing the necessary capabilities, the task boundary would be set to have the service provider perform most of the information processing tasks. This could even extend to creating a knowledge-intensive "super-service" where tasks usually performed by the customer are done by the service provider. An example of this would be an accountant who takes on the organization of the client's documents and records as well as tax preparation. But by being flexible in setting the task boundary for different clients, service providers can appeal to micro-segments of the market with different value calculations. This results in task boundaries that span the gamut from self-service to super-service.

In the next chapter, we look in more depth at capabilities—the foundation for value co-creation as shown in Figure 3.2—and how service providers and customers work together to unlock each other's value co-creation potential. Based on the insights from the current chapter, capabilities are identified that reduce information transfer costs (i.e., information stickiness) and allow the core value-creating activities to be done by the party who provides the most value. Then we move on to how value co-creation can be enhanced even more by reducing the information processing costs themselves through further capability-building. But before ending the chapter, we briefly return to Figure 4.1 and extend it beyond information flows between the service provider and customer to also include the role of the service provider's suppliers in the design of knowledge-intensive service processes.

Generalizing to the Service Supply Chain

The focus of this chapter has been on information flows between the service provider and the customer. However, the service provider can, and often does, outsource tasks to upstream suppliers in the service supply chain. But this just switches the service provider's role to that of a customer, with its supplier as the service provider. And, of course, for many services (such as health care), customers interact with a service network, including providers and other public and private resources, such as information available online, family, and friends.[23] But even with multiple service provider, customer, and supplier relationships, the recommendations for designing knowledge-intensive service processes in Box 4.2 still hold; however, value co-creation would now depend on multiple information processing and transfer costs among three or more parties.

When considering the entire service supply chain, the service process design involves the determination not only of the task boundaries

---

[23]Sweeney, Danaher, and McColl-Kennedy (2015).

between the customer and each service provider but also between service providers and their supplier(s). Looking back to the example of legal document search in Box 2.2, legal firms are increasingly outsourcing this activity to dedicated suppliers with much lower information processing costs. However, initial information transfer costs are high as the law firm and document search firm teams convey and absorb what is often tacit knowledge of the service needs and product capabilities. Consequently, law firms tend to work closely with one document search supplier, which reduces information transfer costs in the long term. By shifting the service process boundary so that the previously labor-intensive document search tasks are outsourced, legal professionals can focus on the value-added task of analyzing evidence from a structured set of digital documents. As a result, each party is doing what it does best—with lower total information processing and transfer costs and increased value co-creation.

Other information-based activities can be done more inexpensively and with better quality if the service provider outsources the task rather than performing it themselves. Many information technology (IT) departments are moving at least some tasks, such as data backup and disaster recovery, to managed service providers (MSPs).[24] Service level agreements that specify the service to be performed and expected performance levels reduce the information transfer costs involved in managing the relationship. As in the case of document search for law firms, outsourcing specific tasks to an MSP can enable the IT department to enhance value by focusing on providing value-added services for their firm or clients with lower costs. Small firms with limited IT resources, in particular, are benefiting from the scale and expertise of an MSP.

Taking the cost and quality benefits of specialization even further, service providers are accessing and suppliers are performing "hyperspecialized" knowledge tasks, often by taking advantage of the scale and low information transfer costs of the Internet.[25] For example, Topcoder divides its clients' IT projects into small pieces and aggregates demand

---

[24]Csaplar (2012).
[25]Malone, Laubacher, and Johns (2011).

for specific tasks, thereby enabling individuals in its network of 300,000 developers from more than 200 countries to more narrowly specialize and yet have plenty of work. In turn, this specialization allows Topcoder to charge its clients much less while providing high-quality results. Other firms such as Amazon's Mechanical Turk broker micro-tasks paying only a few pennies per task. Overall, lower information processing and transfer costs are shifting the task boundary toward outsourcing of ever smaller knowledge tasks.

CHAPTER 5

Unlocking Capabilities

Chapters 3 and 4 laid out a path for unlocking value co-creation through service process design—first for services, in general, and then for knowledge-intensive services, in particular. We now look more closely at the underlying capabilities that are the ultimate source of this value.

Both service providers and customers contribute resources—themselves, information, technologies, materials—to the service process that embody the knowledge, skills, and abilities (KSAs) of the participants in the service supply chain. These resources—both individually and linked together—form the capabilities embedded in the service process design that drive value. For example, knowledge-intensive service professionals such as healthcare providers, attorneys, and consultants have domain-specific KSAs that comprise core capabilities of their service processes. Professionals with high levels of KSAs relevant to the service tasks (which include not only their technical training but also other KSAs such as relational skills) are considered to be more capable. The same is true of technology resources that are part of the service process design; functionalities (i.e., capabilities) add value if they generate benefits, lower costs, or both. Pooled KSAs of resources linked together (e.g., a surgical team with supporting technologies and procedures) form process-level capabilities that can be greater than the sum of individual capabilities.

It follows, then, that by improving current capabilities and developing new ones, the realized value from the service delivery process can be ratcheted up. Although there are a number of approaches to enhancing capabilities, our primary focus will be on how the resources of the service provider and customer can be integrated to "unlock" capabilities. In other words, how can the service provider and customers work together to make each other more capable service value co-creators?

Chapter 2 introduced three important trends that are transforming the service process design landscape: the rapid pace of technology-enabled service innovation, the expanded role of the customer, and the increasing use of service inventory. One of the reasons these trends have had such a significant impact on service process design is that they play a key part in unlocking capabilities and boosting value co-creation. At first blush it might seem that it is only service providers who are unlocking customer capabilities by incorporating innovative technologies into the service process to enable customers to take on new tasks (thereby shifting the service process boundary) or perform existing tasks faster, better, and cheaper. We have seen many examples of this throughout the book, including different types of self-service technologies. But it turns out that the street runs both ways—customers can and do positively affect service provider capabilities. For example, by providing personal information, customers help to create service inventory—and service provider capabilities—that enable providers to offer customers more individualized service experiences.

In this chapter, we will revisit each of the three trends and delve into their impact on process capabilities in more detail. But before moving on, let's look deeper at what "unlocking" capabilities mean and how we can assess their impact on value.

How Can We Tell if Capabilities Have Been Unlocked?

To answer this question, we return to the capability-building panel in the value co-creation measurement model in Table 3.1. Recall that as the foundation for value co-creation in Figure 3.2, capabilities support the firm's strategy and drive current and future firm, customer, and employee service value. These benefits result from investments in building the capabilities of individual and linked process resources. Thus, "unlocking capabilities" consists of adding to the stock of KSAs embodied in the process resources—people, technology, and information—to enhance the benefits as shown in the capability-building panel.

Because capabilities are composed of the resources' KSAs, it would seem that the easiest way to measure the capabilities of process resources is to directly gauge the level of their KSAs. One of the measures in the capability-building panel in Table 3.1 is, in fact, the level of KSAs. But capabilities only add value if they are relevant to the service process; as we noted earlier, in their role as co-producers, customer KSAs tend to be more variable than those of employees and may be irrelevant in terms of the tasks they are being asked to do. So in addition to directly measuring KSAs, it is important to tie capabilities back to the effect they have on value co-creation. In other words, to what extent do they support the firm's short-term and long-term strategy and increase the benefits, reduce the costs, or both for the firm, customer, and employees?

We can look to all four panels in Table 3.1—firm service value, customer service value, employee service value, and capability-building—to identify the set of potential benefits that may be impacted when building capabilities and as a guide for determining which capabilities to build. For example, what is or would be the effect of unlocking capabilities on revenue, internal service quality, or the performance dimensions of delivery speed, quality, flexibility, and innovation? Table 3.1 provides a sample of measures associated with these benefits that can be used for evaluating capabilities.

On the cost side, we draw on the insights from the previous chapter and generalize the four information transfer and processing costs of knowledge-intensive services to a broader range of service processes by including both physical and information processing costs. Reductions in the total information transfer costs and processing costs not only increase value in-and-of themselves but also influence who should do what (i.e., the task boundaries) in the service delivery system, thereby enabling whoever provides the most value to perform a service task. Automatic teller machines (ATMs) are an example of the lowering of information transfer and customer processing costs that allow some banking services tasks to be shifted to the customer with a net increase in value due to lower overall costs and the additional benefit of the convenience of the self-service channel. Focusing on the participants in the service delivery process, unlocking capabilities then involves enabling the customer, the service provider, or both, to perform existing service tasks better and/or perform new tasks. This occurs by: (a) making the tasks easier (by incorporating the capabilities of other process resources—such as ATMs—in the service process design), and/or (b) improving the participants' KSAs (e.g., through training). In the remainder of this chapter, we will see how either the service provider or the customer can lead the way, while recognizing that the unlocking of capabilities is truly a joint effort.

Unlocking of Capabilities within the Firm

Employers have long understood the importance of developing and improving the KSAs of their employees. Talent management processes starting with recruitment, staffing, and on-boarding for new employees, and continuing with ongoing training, help acclimate employees to the company and its culture while providing the necessary KSAs to be effective value co-creators. But there is a growing recognition that employees add value not only through KSAs that affect their individual performance but also through their collaborative contribution to the organization with their formal and informal networks.[1] Employees with high "network effectiveness" KSAs are able to bring together ideas and resources from inside and outside the firm and move them across organizational boundaries to where they are needed. And employers are actively helping employees develop and cultivate their networks through internal socialization processes and technologies. For example, Slack is an employee collaboration and communication platform where team members work together, exchange ideas, and build connections.[2] Similarly, Nationwide Mutual Insurance Company, a large U.S.-based insurer, employs an internal collaboration platform that matches the expertise of employees throughout the company to business challenges.[3] Using this internal collaboration tool, customer service representatives can reduce the time to resolve a difficult customer issue from hours or days to minutes. Viewed through the prism of "unlocking capabilities," these platforms are adding value, in part, by reducing information stickiness and lowering information transfer costs.

We have already touched on "human + machine" approaches—such as cobots—that "combine employees with ever more powerful technologies to create value"[4] For example, some venture capital (VC) firms are supplementing the judgment of their employees with AI and machine-learning tools for identifying promising investment opportunities.[5]

[1]Schweer et al. (2012).
[2]Slack (2020).
[3]Kiron et al. (2012).
[4]Brynjolfsson and McAfee (2012).
[5]Hernandez et al. (2019)

Besides enhancing the efficiency and scale of the evaluation process, these algorithms can help avoid human biases in the decision-making process and diversify the VC investment pool. As another example, Assurant Solutions, a firm that offers credit insurance and debt protection products, brought in mathematicians and actuaries to study their call center operations. Although their call center was already optimized to route calls to employee subject matter specialists, a further analysis of call center data revealed that certain representatives were more successful with specific types of customers—regardless of the particular service need. By automatically routing customers to customer service representatives who had historically done well with that type of a customer, Assurant's historical customer retention rate of 16 percent nearly tripled.[6] Companies such as AT&T are taking this concept even further by employing AI to pair customers and call center agents based on customers' speech and behavior patterns. If the software detects a customer is getting angrier, for example, it reroutes the customer to an agent skilled in conflict de-escalation.[7]

Although not limited to service firms, the rapid pace of technology innovation and access to Big Data has had a profound impact on the service provider tasks and information and physical flows between the service providers and their service supply chain partners. The medical, call center, fraud detection, invoice and payroll processing, and text and speech analytics technologies described in Chapter 2 are employer-provided resources that are integrated with employees as part of the service process design. As employees leverage the capabilities of these technology resources, their capabilities too are unlocked, enabling them to provide better service in less time and at a lower cost.

A final example of a technology acquired by an employer to improve the KSAs of its employees is Oracle's Field Service Cloud, a cloud-based mobile workforce management solution, which has been implemented by firms such as Belgian cable operator VOO and satellite TV provider DISH Network.[8] Using predictive and self-learning technologies, Field Service Cloud can schedule thousands of field technicians and optimize route planning in real time. This allows service technicians to more

---

[6]Brynjolfsson and McAfee (2012); Hopkins and Brokaw (2011).
[7]Terlep (2019).
[8]Oracle (2020).

accurately predict appointment arrival windows, increase the number of installations and repairs per day, and reduce customer waiting times. This, in turn, increases customer satisfaction while improving operational efficiencies and reducing costs.

Not only are firms actively taking steps to unlock the capabilities of their employees but advances in technology and the expanded role of the customer have both enabled and motivated service providers to turn their attention to unlocking the capabilities of their customers as well. We next look at how these efforts can boost value co-creation by increasing benefits, reducing costs, and shifting task boundaries.

Service Providers Unlock Customer Capabilities

When service providers use their resources to unlock customer capabilities, the end result is usually a shift in the task boundary toward more self-service. From the service provider's perspective, the motivation is often cost reduction—essentially "outsourcing" service provider tasks to the customer. But these reductions in service provider processing costs often come with other changes—that is, increases or decreases in customer processing costs, information transfer costs, and benefits—all of which must be considered when deciding whether and how to apply service provider resources to unlock customer capabilities (Box 5.1).

Fortunately, service providers have a number of tools at their disposal to help customers become more capable co-producers—tools that not only increase the benefits but also decrease overall costs. The 24/7 convenience and ease of use of ATMs and online retailing are obvious benefits for customers, but self-service technologies can offer additional benefits as well. In Chapter 2, we described Pursuant Health's kiosks equipped with healthcare screening and educational tools. These kiosks, located in high-traffic retail settings, are certainly convenient—and also enable individuals to be more actively involved in their own health care. Taking this yet further are the self-service medical technologies that allow patients to monitor and even treat chronic conditions. But the viability of these technologies hinges on their ability to reduce information transfer costs from the service provider to the customer and keep customer processing

Box 5.1

Unlocking customer capabilities through field support services

Manufacturers are increasingly bundling value-added services with their products in what is referred to as "servitization." In fact, a wealth of opportunities for unlocking customer capabilities and boosting value on the benefit side of the service value equation can be found in these services. Traditional manufacturers such as IBM and Xerox have transitioned to selling business solutions rather than equipment and are deriving an ever larger share of their revenues and, in some cases, a majority of their profits through the service component of their product–service offerings. And as hardware and software are becoming increasingly complex, these firms are finding that customer capabilities do not always keep pace with the available functionality of their products. (This might sound familiar to anyone who has tried to use the office copier recently!) As a result, even though the benefits of these technologies continue to grow, the gap between the potential value and the customer's ability to extract this value is actually widening.

Firms that provide maintenance and repair services for their own or other original equipment manufacturer (OEM) products—for example, Pitney Bowes, Xerox, Symantec, and Nokia—are attempting to close this gap by changing their model of field service support. The role of field service technicians is evolving from one in which they maintain or fix products at the customer site to also working directly with customers to better understand their needs and increase the benefits, and value, customers realize from these products by closing the gap. By taking on an additional educational role and helping to unlock customers' product usage capabilities, the customer not only extracts more of the potential value from the products but service providers also better justify their own value, which is important when it is time for customers to renew service contracts.

costs under control. The easier these technologies are to explain and use, the more value comes from moving these tasks to the customer. Applications of smart devices in health care have been a game changer in this regard—automating information transfers and much of the information processing as well through Big Data analytics.

Reducing these information transfer costs requires addressing the sources of information stickiness from the service provider to the customer. In the case of Pursuant Health's kiosks, information stickiness stems from the lack of easy access to healthcare services for individuals without insurance or transportation. The location and availability of these kiosks enable people to actually get this information—lessening information stickiness and, consequently, information transfer costs. Similarly, the ProAir Digihaler asthma and COPD management system reduces information transfer costs to near zero by automatically uploading patient data to the product's app, which, in turn, processes the data and provides individualized information back to the patient for self-monitoring. Because the app is designed to be transparent and easy to use, patient processing costs are also considerably reduced.

When service providers need to transfer the same information repeatedly to different customers, they have strong incentives to "unstick" the information. One of the most common technology-enabled tools the service provider uses to reduce information stickiness and unlock customer capabilities is the frequently asked questions (FAQs) screen on a company's website. FAQs enable customer self-service for many common service needs.

Although technologies have been instrumental in reducing information transfer and processing costs, the example of the public cloud infrastructure service provider in Box 2.3 demonstrates that these costs can be reduced by direct service provider-to-customer interactions as well. When the service provider "trains" customers on the basic features of the system, both customer and service provider processing costs go down—the former because customers better understand how to use these features, and the latter because customers have fewer questions. As a result, overall costs are reduced by "employing" customers who are efficient and effective in their co-producer role. Of course, customer training can take a variety of forms. Absent interpersonal interactions in technology-mediated services, customer training for self-service is necessarily technology-based. For example, eBay has detailed instructions on how to list and sell items, as well as guidelines for expected behavior during transactions. Clear expectations for customer responsibilities, combined with customer training, provide a focus and a means for unlocking the right customer capabilities to enhance value co-creation.

Throughout the book are many more examples like these where service provider resources—people, technologies, and information—are expanding the capabilities of customers as value co-creators. By reducing service provider-to-customer information transfer costs, customers can now perform service process tasks that were once the sole province of the service providers. And by making self-service tasks easier and increasing the KSAs of the customers, the service task boundary can be readily shifted to optimize value co-creation.

Before ending this section, we present one last example of unlocking customer capabilities, where customer capabilities are measured in microseconds. The New York Stock Exchange (NYSE) opened a new data center in 2010 in Mahwah, NJ that offers a limited amount of colocation space for trading firms seeking high-speed access to the center's servers—termed "matching machines"—that match buy and sell orders and provide updated pricing information.[9] For low-latency traders (i.e., where trading algorithms require firms to react to market events and arbitrage opportunities with lightning speed), microseconds are often the difference between a profitable and unprofitable trade. As a result, more quickly accessing the resources of the NYSE through colocation unlocks the response time capabilities of the trading firms. Colocation reduces service provider-to-customer information stickiness, while increasing the profits of the trading firms and providing a revenue source for the NYSE—all contributors to value co-creation.

While technology-enabled service innovations are certainly contributors to the unlocking of customer capabilities, these and other innovations are also enabling customers to unlock the capabilities of service providers. Customer-provided information to build service inventory, in particular, takes a technology-enabled service innovation and combines it

---

[9]Miller (2010).

with customer resources to improve service provider capabilities. Regarding the service products themselves, customers have contributed in a big way to new service development and the unlocking of service provider capabilities to better meet customer needs.

Customers Unlock Service Provider Capabilities

Service Inventory Revisited

Chapter 2 introduced the concept of "service inventory" as the portion of the service work that has been performed and stored before the customer arrives. Undifferentiated provider-created service inventory (e.g., Google Finance, WebMD, and online grocers) facilitates customer self-service; in other words, it unlocks customer capabilities to create and track individual financial portfolios, gather information on their medical conditions, and put together their grocery lists.

However, customer-specific service inventory relies on information provided by the customer, either actively or passively, to unlock service provider capabilities to deliver a more personalized service. Prior to the implementation of processes and technologies for easily collecting customer data, this information most certainly would have been described as sticky. For example, the remote monitoring technologies from earlier chapters allow data on the state of customer equipment to be automatically sent to the service provider, reducing the burden on the customer to accurately convey equipment maintenance and repair needs. By unsticking this information, the service inventory in a remote monitoring database enables service providers to offer customers additional benefits such as proactive service before equipment failure and better focused (and faster) service if the equipment does fail.

The more interactions with the customer (either interpersonal—as in Ritz-Carlton's Mystique CRM system or when speaking with a call center employee—or through technology mediators such as IVR systems or smart devices), the more opportunities to unstick and collect customer-specific information. This creates a positive value feedback loop where service providers can further modify the service experience and build customer relationships, which then leads to more interactions, more service process customization, better customer relationships, and so on.

The customer-provided information that helps to unlock service provider capabilities can be acquired in a number of different ways. Of course, many customers volunteer personal information, from creating a profile with an online retailer to using loyalty cards, or enable it to be collected automatically through smart devices. But more and more service providers are collecting customer "data exhaust," such as their clickstream patterns, whether or not customers are aware of it. Firms also buy or derive psychographic information such as age, income, and assets that is not provided directly by customers. All this customer information can then be merged with other databases (e.g., using collaborative filtering to match customer characteristics to other users and their characteristics—as Netflix and Amazon are doing) to further customize the service product and process activities (Box 5.2).

Box 5.2

"True Fit" improves customer service for online retailers

Anyone who has ever shopped for clothes knows that sizing can be an enigma because of the lack of standardization in the clothing industry. This is especially problematic when shopping online.[10] Nearly half of online shoppers engage in "bracketing"—buying multiple sizes with the intent of returning ones that do not fit.[11] Not only is this time-consuming and frustrating for customers, but product returns add significant expenses for retailers. To better deal with this sizing problem, fashion retailers such as Macy's and Nordstrom are asking customers to help them provide better service through "True Fit," a service being offered for online purchases.[12] Customers create a profile with their age, height, weight, and body shape. But the key to True Fit is that customers also identify the brands, styles, and sizes of clothes that fit well from their own closet. The True Fit Genome platform then compares the customer's profile to their database of garment

---

[10]Kapner (2019).
[11]Berthene (2019).
[12]True Fit (2020).

specifications for a large number of fashion labels and recommends a size for garments selected by the customer—and even makes suggestions for other garments that would fit well. Because True Fit keeps track of what consumers buy and what they return, the updated (service inventory) profile, which is portable to any participating retailer, enables the algorithm to make more precise recommendations over time. Although True Fit requires customers to spend a few minutes setting up their profiles, the program is designed to dramatically reduce information stickiness about customer sizing and help the retailer get the right product in the right size to the right customer. By decreasing the time and cost of product returns for both the customer and retailer, True Fit is designed to boost value co-creation by accurately "tailoring" the service process to each customer, all while lowering overall costs.

The growing availability of social, mobile, and location (SoMoLo) customer information continues to be transformative for personalizing services; the amount of data, as well as its depth and breadth, dwarfs other data collection channels.[13] Recognizing the tremendous value of SoMoLo information, in 2010, Walmart acquired Kosmix, a startup that had developed a technology for tracking vast amounts of social media data, to form Walmart Labs. One of the products to emerge from this new entity was Polaris, the search engine powering Walmart.com and the company's mobile apps, which incorporates a customer's actual search and purchasing behavior to "train" the system to personalize subsequent customer searches.[14] It also pulls in social signals (e.g., Facebook "likes" and Twitter "tweets") to help return better search results. And the Walmart app's Store Assistant allows customers to create a shopping list, calculate the cost of their basket before setting foot in the store, and crosses off and adds items while shopping. It also provides turn-by-turn directions to enable customers to more quickly and easily find items in a Walmart store (all of Walmart's stores are geofenced). In addition, just as Samsung is

---

[13]Davenport, Dalle Mule, and Lucker (2011).

[14]The examples of Walmart Labs technologies are from Marvin (2016) and the Walmart Labs (2020).

monitoring social media to target the product service needs of a customer group, Walmart Labs can mine social media to develop profiles of neighborhoods that help guide the stocking of store inventories.[15] In each of these cases, service inventory is being created to perform and store service work—in the form of customized online and in-store product search and targeted product stocking—even before the customer enters the service system. But while customer data are expanding the capabilities of service providers to offer increasingly customized services, legal and ethical costs associated with its use, especially for passively collected customer information, must be balanced against the benefits.

Customer-Driven Service Innovation

Recall the "open innovation" process that leverages ideas and technologies, not only within the firm but also increasingly outside the firm, to drive internal service innovation development. One source of these ideas and technologies is the customers themselves. After all, if customers can help service providers to better meet their needs, everyone benefits. But when information about customer needs is sticky, as it often is with functionally novel services, the difficulty and cost of transferring this information from the customer to the service provider is high. Thus, innovative customers (i.e., "lead users") may take matters into their own hands and devise a way to self-provide the needed service.[16] For firms paying attention, these lead user innovations essentially broadcast, and unstick, the underlying customer needs information. By providing a template for a service product and delivery process that meets their own needs, lead users are unlocking the capabilities of the service provider to offer a service that potentially adds value not only for that particular customer but also across their customer base. While the example of the artificial pancreas for Type I diabetes from Chapter 2 is one of many self-provided medical innovations, customers have also been a surprisingly common source of innovation for banking services (Box 5.3).

---

[15]Geron (2011).
[16]Oliveira and von Hippel (2011).

Box 5.3

Customers as innovators in banking services

A study of computerized financial services introduced by U.S. commercial banks from 1975 to 2010 found that 55 percent of the core corporate services and 44 percent of the core retail services now being offered by banks were originally developed and self-provided in electronic form by user firms, individuals, or nonbank service providers.[17] An early version of the payroll processing services first commercialized by banks in the 1980s was developed back in the 1950s for their own use by J. Lyons & Co., a large baking and catering company in the United Kingdom. In the early 1980s, tech-savvy customers developed computer programs to aggregate their own account information across multiple institutions. Commercial versions of this service did not appear until the late 1990s.

Even though users were the source of about half of the computerized financial services innovations in the study, a number of these services also had self-provided precursors that were manually implemented. Of the financial services that had manual precursors, the vast majority (92 percent of corporate banking services and 80 percent of retail banking services) was developed by user firms and individuals. For example, a "sweep account" (in which a customer's funds are moved among various accounts at a financial institution to maximize interest yields) was pioneered and performed manually by both business and individual users (i.e., customers issued transaction-specific instructions for moving money between noninterest-bearing checking accounts and interest-bearing savings accounts). Another example is the popular "keep the change" service, in which customers authorize their bank to automatically round up debit card purchases to the nearest dollar and transfer the difference from their checking to savings account. Manual versions that predate the bank-provided service range from customers who round up the amount of a check when entering the transaction in their checkbook register to "change jars" in homes. These functionalities were later built into banking software (e.g., Bank of America first introduced a "keep the change" service in 2005), enhanced, and offered to customers in a convenient, digital form.

---

[17]This box is based on a research study by Oliveira and von Hippel (2011).

Summary: Customers as a Key to Unlocking Service Provider Capabilities

When customers provide information about themselves and their service needs, they are adding to the stock of knowledge possessed by the service provider. In some cases, service providers use this knowledge to create service inventory and deliver more personalized services. In other cases, the knowledge is an awareness of new opportunities for meeting customer needs. In addition, customer innovators are contributing to the skills and abilities of service providers through self-developed "prototypes" on which the providers' own products and processes can be patterned. In each of these cases, it is clear that customers—by enhancing the KSAs of the service provider—are positively impacting the internal service quality and employee service value that lead to value co-creation (as in Figure 3.1). This is true regardless of whether the ultimate service delivery model is self-service mobile banking (e.g., customers were using Internet-enabled cell phones to conduct mobile banking before banks created mobile banking apps appropriate for cell phone screens[18]), full-service sweep account services, or super-service remote monitoring.

But, in reality, customers and service providers do not unlock capabilities in isolation. In fact, the real power of the concept lies in the synergies achieved when both parties work together to improve their joint capabilities.

Capability Synergies

Capability Synergies in Service Product Innovation

The example of customers as banking services innovators in Box 5.3 is presented as one in which customers are unlocking the capabilities of service providers in two ways—by unsticking customer needs information and by self-providing a version of the service that can be used as a launching point for the providers' own development efforts. Once the service provider recognizes the potential value of the innovation, they have a strong incentive to improve on the original innovation before offering it to all their customers. So while customer innovators initially unlock

---

[18]Oliveira and von Hippel (2011).

service provider capabilities, the service providers, in turn, bring their own resources to bear to design a comparable service that is faster, better, and cheaper than the one it is replacing. While some of these banking services are now performed by the service provider, others are offered through a self-service channel—ATMs, online and mobile banking, and telephone banking. These technologies and service processes have unlocked the capabilities of the rest of the customer base to perform self-service. This is what is meant by "capability synergies"—the unlocking of capabilities by one party fosters a self-reinforcing cycle that enhances the capabilities and value co-creation potential of both customers and service providers.

In retailing, the Hero omni-channel platform helps online shoppers better meet their needs—but with a different approach than TrueFit for generating capability synergies.[19] When a customer shopping online types in a question on the retailer's website or mobile app, Hero geolocates them and sends a message to an associate in the closest physical store. In addition to responding to the customer's question, an associate can invite online customers to the store to see the product in person. As with TrueFit, the impact on returns is substantial—a 40 percent reduction in product return rates—along with an 8 percent to 10 percent increase in purchases. Enabling a customer to conveniently gather information before making a purchase promotes capability synergies. The service provider unlocks the capabilities of the customer to make more informed buying decisions, while the direct interaction with the customer unlocks the capabilities of the service provider to get the right product in the right size to the right customer.

Another model of service product development is one in which service providers and customers work collaboratively to co-create the service product. As with customer-led service innovations, a collaborative approach promotes the development of capabilities by both parties, but with some differences. Take, for example, a complex product such as a health insurance plan.[20] Firms either sell standard plans or allow customer groups to work with the providers to create a customized plan by adding and modifying certain elements. Just like with the banking

---

[19]Grewal et al. (2020).
[20]This example is based on a research study by Kumar and Telang (2011).

services introduced by customers, this collaborative process reduces information stickiness regarding customer needs. But it also reduces information stickiness from the insurer to the customer; the joint effort to customize the product fulfills an educational function that familiarizes the customers with the features of their plan. By making information transfers less sticky, the insurer is able to provide a product that is a better fit for individual customers. This, in turn, reduces product uncertainty for the customer, and according to a study of a U.S. health insurance firm, has resulted in 21 percent fewer calls to the insurer's call center for clarification of the product's coverage. Thus, improving service provider and customer capabilities (i.e., knowledge of customer needs and knowledge of the product, respectively) translates into greater value co-creation; the customer benefits from a more customized service product and both service provider and customer information processing costs are reduced because of fewer calls to the insurer's call center.

Capability Synergies with Service Inventory

Capability synergies are also evident in processes that incorporate service inventory. Whereas undifferentiated service inventory enables customers to tailor the service to meet their own needs (i.e., service providers unlocking customer capabilities) and customer-specific service inventory helps service providers deliver personalized services (i.e., customers unlocking service provider capabilities), in each case, capability-building goes both ways. Technologies for collecting customer information are becoming increasingly sophisticated, with customer data acquired through store, call center, online, social media, and mobile channels. These technologies allow customers to provide more—and more specific—information to service providers. With this customer information, service providers can not only move "toward an environment of personalized interactions"[21] but also modify their undifferentiated service inventory (e.g., data and analytical tools) to better meet customer needs. And the cycle continues—as firms attempt to further align their services with customer needs, customer-provided information becomes more useful for

---

[21]Cunnane (2012).

evaluating the success of these efforts and driving improvements to the service processes.

But by reducing the stickiness of so much customer information, firms have opened up the "proverbial fire hose of data"[22]—enormous quantities of data that, at the same time, is growing increasingly complex. Fortunately, a number of business intelligence (BI) platforms are available for making sense of this "torrent of structured and unstructured data,"[23] either as stand-alone software applications or embedded in existing business applications such as CRM systems[24] and smart networks. Using BI platforms for joint capability-building, the opportunities for value co-creation are virtually limitless.

The Self-Reinforcing Cycle of Capability Synergies

It should be apparent by now that when service providers help customers to be better co-producers, they are also enriching their own capabilities as service providers. The same is true for customers; by unlocking the capabilities of service providers with their innovations and information, they are gaining KSAs that enable them to take on tasks formerly performed by service providers. Let's return to field support services, self-service medical technologies, and consulting services to see how capability synergies work for these services.

When field service technicians work with customers to close the gap between the potential value of their hardware or software and the customer's current realized value, it goes without saying that customer KSAs improve. But while furthering their own capabilities, customers are also building service providers' knowledge about what features and functionalities are most beneficial, as well as enabling the technicians to better target their customer education efforts and provide useful feedback to the OEMs. And while self-service medical technologies have allowed patients to take on monitoring and sometimes treatment tasks, the information that patients send back to their medical providers when using the self-service technologies enable the providers to fine-tune or even alter

---

[22]Lock (2012a).
[23]Mehta (2019).
[24]Lock (2012b).

the patient's medical care. Finally, because of the client's central role as a co-producer of the knowledge-based service product, capability syner-gies are an almost universal attribute of consulting services. The back-and-forth exchange of domain-specific and project-specific knowledge between the consultant and client, for example, builds and strengthens the capabilities of each party, especially with recurring services. This is why many instructors (including me) say that they learn as much from their students as the students learn from them.

Capability Synergies in the Service Supply Chain

With advances in social media tools, firms are increasingly adopting a "social business" model (defined as "activities that use social media, social software, and social networks to enable more efficient, effective, and mu-tually useful connections between people, information, and assets"[25]) that extends the concept of capability synergies throughout the service supply chain. For example, SAP, an ERP software company, has created an online community with 2 million plus members that includes customers, part-ners, and SAP employees. In doing so, SAP has unlocked the capabilities of its entire network to provide information and feedback about SAP software and service products—not only back to SAP but also to and from all nodes in their network (e.g., customer-to-customer).[26]

Further, in a trend termed "unsourcing," firms such as TomTom (navigation products and services), Best Buy, Lenovo (computers and technology services), and Logitech (personal computer accessories) have set up online communities to enable peer-to-peer technology support among users.[27] By leveraging the KSAs of their customers, customer sup-port costs are reduced and the customer support capabilities of the entire network are enhanced. Of course, as with any service involving customer co-production, processes must be designed to motivate and ensure the quality of customer co-production. One approach that has been em-ployed by these firms is to monitor activity in the online community and award points for helpful answers. Similar to a rating system, this allows

---

[25]Kiron et al. (2012).
[26]Ibid.
[27]"Outsourcing Is So Passé" (2012).

other customers to identify sources of reliable information and acknowledges the effort of the users providing it.

Summary: Integrating Resources to Unlock Capabilities

Because capabilities are the foundation on which value co-creation is based, capability-building and potential capability synergies should be top-of-mind when designing and executing service processes. Box 5.4 poses a number of questions service process participants should ask to guide decisions about whether and how to integrate resources to unlock capabilities.

Box 5.4

Unlocking capabilities: strategy, value, and setting the task boundary

Before investing in capability-building, service process participants need to determine what capabilities should be unlocked and which process resources should be involved. Based on the frameworks, models, and recommendations for unlocking value co-creation found throughout this book, following are some questions they should be asking in terms of strategy, value, and setting the task boundary:

Strategy: What capabilities are needed to support the firm's current and future strategy? For service processes that rely heavily on customer co-production through self-service, capability-building efforts would be directed toward capabilities that enable the customer to perform their tasks proficiently. Full-service and super-service processes would be more focused on developing service provider capabilities.

Value: How will these capabilities add to firm, customer, and employee service value? What is the expected effect on benefits: revenue, internal service quality, and the performance dimensions of delivery speed, quality, flexibility, and innovation? What is the expected effect on information transfer costs and processing costs? Because value increases when benefits exceed costs, the specific choice of capabilities to develop is guided by their potential impact on current and future value. For example, to offer a more personalized service experience, one approach would be investing in processes or technologies to capture and analyze customer-provided information. Determining if this is the "right" way to unlock the capability of the service provider to customize the service delivery process depends on whether the benefits are greater than the costs (including the "cost" of privacy concerns incurred by the customer). The "connected car" from Chapter 3 is a good example of the challenges of balancing personalization benefits versus customer privacy costs, especially when determining how extensive the associated IoT network should be and who should have access to customer data.

Setting the task boundary: Is the party that can provide the most value capable of performing a service process task? If not, should the relevant capabilities be unlocked by making the task easier? Or should the KSAs themselves be enhanced? In-home self-dialysis incorporates both approaches. The patient receives extensive training on the dialysis process and suppliers continue to roll out machines that are easier to set up, clean, and disinfect. In fact, studies show that the more patients know about their treatment and the more they do on their own, the better they do on dialysis.[28] As another example, financial services innovations introduced by users unlock the capabilities of the service provider to offer a service that creates value across their customer base by providing information on customer needs and a template for the service itself. By making these services available in a fast, accurate, and low-cost digital form, the provider not only adds value for the services they retain but also unlocks the capabilities of the customer to perform self-service for other banking tasks. As a result, capabilities and value co-creation are aligned.

Concluding Remarks

Throughout the book, we have seen how the rapid pace of technology-enabled service innovation, the expanded role of the customer, and the increasing use of service inventory are opening up new possibilities for designing service processes to co-create value. But regardless of the changes in the service process design landscape, the fundamentals of

---

[28]National Kidney Foundation (2020).

how value is created—through the design of service products and delivery processes in which the benefits are perceived to be greater than the costs—are still just as valid as ever.

One of the most important goals of this book is to provide you—the reader—with a roadmap for designing service processes to unlock their value co-creation potential. We start down this path with the value co-creation framework and value co-creation measurement model. They provide a systematic way for service process designers to identify and measure the benefits, costs, trade-offs, and synergies that drive value co-creation. Building on this general approach to designing service processes are additional recommendations specific to designers of knowledge-intensive service processes. And underlying any approach to designing service processes for value co-creation is the unlocking of service provider and customer capabilities. Determining what capabilities to unlock, and how to do it, provides the foundation for value co-creation that concludes our journey.

In this book, we've focused primarily on the interactions between service providers and customers as value co-creators. But we have also looked to the broader service supply chain, where services outsourcing and crowdsourcing, for example, are impacting the value equation. This focus extends to the unlocking of capabilities through the integration of service provider and customer resources or by accessing resources in the service supply chain. However, the online communities for peer-to-peer technology support set up by TomTom, Best Buy, and Lenovo entail customers unlocking the capabilities of *other* customers to better meet their own service needs. In fact, this example shows that many of the same technologies (e.g., the Internet, social media, and mobile devices) that are helping to unlock value among the service provider, customer, and supply chain partners are finding applications outside the usual value co-creation channels.

One final note: You and I are service co-producers—you by reading the book and I by writing it. But I hope we have gone beyond co-production to the level of true value co-creation as you apply the ideas in this book to designing your own service processes.

References

6 River Systems. 2020. "Office Depot Improves Safety and Energizes Workforce with Collaborative Robots." www.6river.com/office-depot/, (date accessed April 20, 2020).

Allon, G., A. Federgruen, and M. Pierson. 2011. "How Much Is a Reduction of Your Customers' Wait Worth? An Empirical Study of the Fast-Food Drive-Thru Industry Based on Structural Estimation Models." *Manufacturing & Service Operations Management* 13, no. 4, pp. 489–507.

Anand, K. S., M. F. Pac, and S. Veeraraghavan. 2011. "Quality-Speed Conundrum: Trade-Offs in Customer-Intensive Services." *Management Science* 57, no. 1, pp. 40–56.

Antorini, Y. M., A. M. Muniz, Jr., and T. Askildsen. 2012. "Collaborating with Customer Communities: Lessons from the Lego Group." *MIT Sloan Management Review* 53, no. 3, pp. 73–9.

Anupindi, R., S. Chopra, S. D. Deshmukh, J. A. Van Mieghem, and E. Zemel, 2012. *Managing Business Process Flows.* 3rd ed. Upper Saddle River, NJ: Pearson Education.

Apple Maps. 2020. www.apple.com/ios/maps/, (date accessed April 13, 2020).

Arizona Judicial Branch. 2020. "Self Service Forms." www.azcourts.gov/selfservicecenter/Forms/Pro-Hac-Vice, (date accessed May 13, 2020).

Bellos, I., and S. Kavadias. 2019. "When Should Customers Control Service Delivery? Implications for Service Design." *Production and Operations Management* 28, no. 4, pp. 890–907.

Berthene, A. September 12, 2019. "Sizing Issue is a Top Reason Shoppers Return Online Orders." *Digital Commerce 360.* www.digitalcommerce360.com/2019/09/12/sizing-issue-is-a-top-reason-shoppers-return-online-orders/, (date accessed March 27, 2020).

Bettencourt, L. A., A. L Ostrom, S. W. Brown, and R. I. Roundtree. 2002. "Client Co-Production in Knowledge-Intensive Business Services." *California Management Review* 44, no. 4, pp. 100–28.

Bitner, M. J., A. L. Ostrom, and M. L. Meuter. 2002. "Implementing Successful Self-Service Technologies." *Academy of Management Executive* 16, no. 4, pp. 96–108.

Blackboard. 2020. www.blackboard.com, (date accessed April 10, 2020).

Blackboard Infographic. 2020. https://blog.blackboard.com/infographic-march-covid-19-impact-on-education/, (date accessed April 10, 2020).

Blandino, S. 2016. "How the Ritz-Carlton Delivers Exceptional Customer Service." http://stephenblandino.com/2016/07/how-the-ritz-carlton-delivers-exceptional-customer-service.html, (date accessed April 17, 2020).

Bray, H. April 24, 2020a. "The Robot Will See You Now." *Boston Globe*. www.bostonglobe.com/2020/04/23/business/robot-will-see-you-now/, (date accessed April 24, 2020).

Bray, H. February 11, 2020b. "In Smart Apartments, is Tenants' Privacy for Rent? *Boston Globe*. www.bostonglobe.com/2020/02/11/business/smart-apartments-is-tenants-privacy-rent/, (date accessed February 13, 2020).

Briggs, E., S. Deretti, and H. T. Kato. 2020. "Linking Organizational Service Orientation to Retailer Profitability: Insights from the Service-Profit Chain." *Journal of Business Research* 107, pp. 271–8.

Brynjolfsson, E., and A. McAfee. 2012. "Winning the Race with Ever-Smarter Machines." *MIT Sloan Management Review* 53, no. 2, pp. 53–60.

Buell, R. W., and M. I. Norton. 2011. "The Labor Illusion: How Operational Transparency Increases Perceived Value." *Management Science* 57, no. 9, pp. 1564–79.

Burke, L. November 4, 2019. "Your Interview with AI." *Inside Higher Ed*. www.insidehighered.com/news/2019/11/04/ai-assessed-job-interviewing-grows-colleges-try-prepare-students?utm_source=Inside+Higher+Ed&utm_campaign=0c3d8f47d8-DNU_2019_COPY_01&utm_medium=email&utm_term=0_1fcbc04421-0c3d8f47d8-197545437&mc_cid=0c3d8f47d8&mc_eid=d9762602af, (date accessed April 5, 2020).

Byrum, J., and A. Bingham. 2016. "Improving Analytics Capabilities through Crowdsourcing." *MIT Sloan Management Review* 57, no. 4, pp. 43–8.

Carlisle, M. March 27, 2020. "How Can You Safely Grocery Shop in the Time of Coronavirus? Here's What Experts Suggest." *Time*. https://time.com/5810782/grocery-store-safety-coronavirus/, (date accessed March 31, 2020).

Campbell, D., and F. X. Frei. 2010. "Cost Structure Customer Profitability and Retention Implications of Self-Service Distribution Channels: Evidence from Customer Behavior in an Online Banking Channel." *Management Science* 56, no. 1, pp. 4–24.

Campbell, C. S., P. P. Maglio, and M. M. Davis. 2011. "From Self-Service to Super-Service: A Resource Mapping Framework for Co-Creating Value by Shifting the Boundary between Provider and Customer." *Information Systems and E-Business Management* 9, no. 2, pp. 173–91.

CDP. 2020. www.cdp.net/en, (date accessed April 3, 2020).

Chesbrough, H. 2011. "Bringing Open Innovation to Services." *MIT Sloan Management Review* 52, no. 2, pp. 85–90.

Chopra, S., and M. A. Lariviere. 2005. "Managing Service Inventory to Improve Performance." *MIT Sloan Management Review* 47, no. 1, pp. 56–63.

Chun, R. 2018. "The Banana Trick and Other Acts of Self-Checkout Thievery." *The Atlantic.* www.theatlantic.com/magazine/archive/2018/03/stealing-from-self-checkout/550940/, (date accessed February 17, 2020).

Cima, R. R., A. Kollengode, J. Clark, S. Pool, C. Weisbrod, G. J. Amstutz, and C. Deschamps. 2011. "Using a Data-Matrix–Coded Sponge Counting System Across a Surgical Practice: Impact After 18 Months." *The Joint Commission Journal on Quality and Patient Safety* 37, no. 2, pp. 51–8.

"Clicking for Gold: How Internet Companies Profit from Data on the Web." 2010. *The Economist* 394(8671), special section, pp. 9–11, February 27.

Cogito. 2020. www.cogitocorp.com/product/, (date accessed April 23, 2020).

Conexiom. 2020. https://conexiom.com/, (date accessed April 23, 2020).

Connected Technology Solutions. 2020. https://connectedts.com/, (date accessed May 21, 2020).

Cooley, D. December 5, 2014. "IBM Wants to Put Your Parked Car to Work." *Smart Cities Council.* https://smartcitiescouncil.com/article/ibm-wants-put-your-parked-car-work, (date accessed April 14, 2020).

Core77 Design Awards. 2014. www.core77designawards.com/2014/recipients/pillpack-pharmacy-simplified/, (date accessed May 6, 2020).

Csaplar, D. January 2012. *Managed Service Providers: A Stepping Stone to the Public Cloud.* Boston, MA: Aberdeen Group.

Cunnane, C. March 2012. *Hyper-Connected Online Retail Personalization: Driving Results with a Customized Experience.* Boston, MA: Aberdeen Group.

Curtis, T. May 3, 2019. "In Praise of Self-Checkouts. *Foundation for Economic Education.* https://fee.org/articles/in-praise-of-self-checkouts/, (date accessed June 22, 2020).

Dale, B. January 23, 2019. "'Decentralized Airbnb' Starts Charging Fees as ICO Model Falters." *Coindesk.* www.coindesk.com/decentralized-airbnb-starts-charging-fees-as-ico-model-falters, (date accessed April 1, 2020).

Davenport, T. H., L. Dalle Mule, and J. Lucker. 2011. "Know What Your Customers Want Before They Do." *Harvard Business Review* 89, no. 12, pp. 84–92.

Davis, M. M., J. Field, and E. Stavrulaki. 2015. "Using Digital Service Inventories to Create Customer Value." *Service Science* 7, no. 2, pp. 83–99.

Davis, M. M., J. C. Spohrer, and P. P. Maglio. 2011. "Guest Editorial: How Technology Is Changing the Design and Delivery of Services." *Operations Management Research* 4, no. 1, pp. 1–5.

De, P., Y. Hu, and S. Rahman. 2010. "Technology Usage and Online Sales: An Empirical Study." *Management Science* 57, no. 11, pp. 1930–45.

De Keyser, A., S. Köcher, L. Alkire, C. Verbeeck, and J. Kandampully. 2019. "Frontline Service Technology Infusion: Conceptual Archetypes and Future Research Directions." *Journal of Service Management* 30, no. 1, pp. 156–83.

DeMonaco, H., P. Oliveira, A. Torrance, C. von Hippel, and E. von Hippel. 2019. "When Patients Become Innovators." *MIT Sloan Management Review* 60, no. 3, pp. 81–8.

Department of Homeland Security. 2018. "Border Surveillance Systems." www.dhs.gov/publication/border-surveillance-systems-bss, (date accessed April 25, 2020).

Dependable Cleaners. 2020. https://dependablecleaners.com/original-home-delivery/, (date accessed April 18, 2020).

Des Marais, A., Y. Zhao, M. Hobbs, V. Sivaraman, L. Barclay, N. T. Brewer, and J. S. Smith. 2018. "Home Self-Collection by Mail to Test for Human Papillomavirus and Sexually Transmitted Infections." *Obstetrics & Gynecology* 132, no. 6, pp. 1412–20.

Digimarc. July 21, 2015. "Digimarc Survey: 88 Percent of U.S. Adults Want Their Retail Checkout Experience to Be Faster." www.digimarc.com/about/news-events/press-releases/2015/07/21/digimarc-survey-88-percent-of-u.s.-adults-want-their-retail-checkout-experience-to-be-faster, (date accessed April 25, 2020).

Domonoske, C. April 13, 2020. "A Pound of Flour to Go? Restaurants Are Selling Groceries Now." *NPR*. www.npr.org/2020/04/13/831635629/a-pound-of-flour-to-go-restaurants-are-selling-groceries-now, (date accessed May 2, 2020).

Dwyer, B. 2019. "Self Checkout: Should you Implement It?" *CardFellow*. www.cardfellow.com/blog/self-checkout-should-you-implement-it/, (date accessed February 17, 2020).

Dzieza, J. February 27, 2020. "How Hard Will the Robots Make Us Work?" *The Verge*. www.theverge.com/2020/2/27/21155254/automation-robots-unemployment-jobs-vs-human-google-amazon, (date accessed April 12, 2020).

Edmund, M. 2015. "When App-licable. Retailers Take to Apps to Enhance Shopper Experience and Collect Data." *Quality Progress* 48, no. 6, pp. 12-14.

Ethiraj, S. K., P. Kale, M. S. Krishnan, and J. V. Singh. 2005. "Where do Capabilities Come from and How Do They Matter? A Study in the Software Service Industry." *Strategic Management Journal* 26, no. 1, pp. 25–45.

Faridi, O. January 7, 2020. "IBM and Farmer Connect Introduce Blockchainbased App that Lets Users Learn about Coffee Beans They've Purchased." *Crowdfund Insider.* www.crowdfundinsider.com/2020/01/156025-ibm-andfarmer-connect-introduce-blockchain-based-app-that-lets-users-learnabout-coffee-beans-theyve-purchased/, (date accessed May 1, 2020).

Fosco, M. March 19, 2019. "A.I. Begins Exercising Power Over Your Home Fitness." *OZY.* www.ozy.com/the-new-and-the-next/a-i-begins-exercising-power-overyour-home-fitness/92613/?utm_term=OZY&utm_source=Sailthru&utm_medium=email&utm_campaign=DailyDose_06012019&utm_content=A, (date accessed April 14, 2020).

Frei, F. X. 2008. "The Four Things a Service Business Must Get Right." *Harvard Business Review* 86, no. 4, pp. 70–80.

Gandhi, S., and E. Gervet. 2016. "Now That Your Products Can Talk, What Will They Tell You?" *MIT Sloan Management Review* 57, no. 3, pp. 49–50.

Gantry Group. September 2002. "Quantifying Your Value Proposition." *Gantry Group Newsletter*, Issue 15. www.gantrygroup.com/images/Newsletter1/News15.html, (date accessed December 30, 2011).

Gaskill, T. 2015. "House Call Overhaul." *Quality Progress* 48, no. 12, pp. 12–14.

Gawande, A. 2010. *The Checklist Manifesto*. New York: Picador.

Geron, T. 2011. "The Fast Data Behind the Coming Apps from @ WalmartLabs." *Forbes*, September 12. www.forbes.com/sites/tomiogeron/2011/09/12/the-fast-data-behind-the-coming-apps-from-walmartlabs/#4764a6171cbb, (date accessed April 25, 2020).

GetHuman Website. 2020. www.gethuman.com/, (date accessed April, 10, 2020).

Glomark-Governan. 2006. *Quantifying Outsourcing Intangible Benefits*. 3rd ed. A Glomark-Governan White Paper. www.glomark-governan.com/images/Glomark_White_Paper_Outsourcing_Intangible_Benefits_Edition_3.pdf, (date accessed April 25, 2020).

Grewal, D., S. M. Noble, A. L. Roggeveen, and J. Nordfalt. 2020. "The Future of In-Store Technology." *Journal of the Academy of Marketing Science* 48, pp. 96–113.

Groupon Q4 2019 Fact Sheet. 2019. https://s22.q4cdn.com/731250486/files/doc_downloads/general/Q4-2019-Fact-Sheet.pdf, (date accessed April 30, 2020).

Groysberg, B., W. Johnson, and E. Lin. 2019. "When to Do When Industry Disruption Threatens Your Career." *MIT Sloan Management Review* 60, no. 3, pp. 57–65.

Guajardo, J. A., M. A. Cohen, S. H. Kim, and S. Netessine. 2012. "Impact of Performance-Based Contracting on Product Reliability: An Empirical Analysis." *Management Science* 58, no. 5, pp. 961–76.

Halder, B. March 24, 2019. "How China's 'Cobot' Revolution Could Transform Automation." *OZY*. www.ozy.com/fast-forward/how-chinas-cobot-revolution-could-transform-automation/93044/, (date accessed April 11, 2020).

Hamacher, A. May 9, 2017. "The Unpopular Rise of Self-Checkouts (and How to Fix Them)." *BBC Future*. www.bbc.com/future/article/20170509-the-unpopular-rise-of-self-checkouts-and-how-to-fix-them, (date accessed January 21, 2020).

Harris, S. 2019. "Machines vs. Cashiers: Why Shoppers Are So Divided over Self-Checkout." *CBC News*. www.cbc.ca/news/business/self-checkout-cashiers-retail-jobs-technology-1.5020299, (date accessed February 17, 2020).

Hart, O. 1995. *Firms, Contracts, and Financial Structure*. Oxford: Oxford University Press.

Hasija, S., Z.-J. M. Shen, and C.-P. Teo. 2020. "Smart City Operations: Modeling Challenges and Opportunities." *Manufacturing & Service Operations Management* 22, no. 1, pp. 203–213.

Hayes, R., G. Pisano, D. Upton, and S. Wheelwright. 2005. *Operations, Strategy, and Technology: Pursuing the Competitive Edge*. Hoboken, NJ: John Wiley & Sons.

Hayes, R. H., and D. M. Upton. 1998. "Operations-Based Strategy." *California Management Review* 40, no. 4, pp. 8–25.

Hedgecock, S. April 15, 2015. "Pharmacy Startup PillPack Could Change the Way America Takes Its Medicine." *Forbes*. www.forbes.com/sites/sarahhedgecock/2015/04/15/this-pharmacy-startup-wants-to-change-the-way-you-take-your-medicine/2/#e20918f67307, (date accessed April 25, 2020).

Hernandez, M., R. Raveendhran, E. Weingarten, and M. Barnett. 2019. "How Algorithms Can Deversity the Startup Pool." *MIT Sloan Management Review* 61, no. 1, pp. 71–7.

Heskett, J. L., T. O. Jones, G. W. Loveman, W. E. Sasser, Jr., and L. A. Schlesinger. 1994. "Putting the Service-Profit Chain to Work." *Harvard Business Review* 72, no. 2, pp. 164–70.

Heskett, J. L., T. O. Jones, G. W. Loveman, W. E. Sasser, Jr., and L. A. Schlesinger. 2008. "Putting the Service-Profit Chain to Work." *Harvard Business Review* 86, nos. 7/8, pp. 118–29.

Hogreve, J., A. Iseke, and K. Derfuss. 2017. "The Service-Profit Chain: A Meta-Analytic Test of a Comprehensive Theoretical Framework." *Journal of Marketing* 81, no. 3, pp. 41–61.

Hopkins, M. S., and L. Brokaw. 2011. "Matchmaking with Math: How Analytics Beats Intuition to Win Customers." *MIT Sloan Management Review* 52, no. 2, pp. 35–41.

Howard, P. W. January 25, 2020. "Fired Salesman Disrupts Car-Buying Industry with Word-of-Mouth 'Concierge' Business." *USA Today.* www.usatoday.com/story/money/cars/2020/01/25/fired-car-salesman-brian-carroll-dealership/4562794002/, (date accessed April 30, 2020).

Hsieh, T. 2010. *Delivering Happiness: A Path to Profits, Passion, and Purpose.* New York: Business Plus.

Huang, M.-H., R. Rust, and V. Maksimovic. 2019. "The Feeling Economy: Managing in the Next Generation of Artificial Intelligence (AI)." *California Management Review* 61, no. 4, pp. 63–85.

IBM (International Business Machine). 2016a. "First-of-a-Kind Program (FOAK)." www.research.ibm.com/FOAK/about.shtml, (date accessed June 25, 2016).

IBM (International Business Machine). 2016b. "IBM and Danish Hospital Pioneer Smarter Patient Records to Improve Patient Care." www-03.ibm.com/press/us/en/pressrelease/26870.wss, (date accessed June 25, 2016).

Idea Connection. October 22, 2009. "Open Innovation: Netflix Prize." www.ideaconnection.com/open-innovation-success/Open-Innovation-Netflix-Prize-00032.html, (date accessed April 4, 2020).

Jolt Consulting Group. 2015. "Internet of Things in Field Service? A Whitepaper." http://joltconsultinggroup.com/internet-of-things-in-field-service-a-whitepaper/, (date accessed April 25, 2020).

Jones, C. October 8, 2015. "PillPack's Single-Dose Packs Makes Juggling Multiple Prescriptions a Snap." *USA Today.* www.usatoday.com/story/money/business/small%20business/2015/09/29/pillpack-makes-juggling-multiple-prescriptions-easy/72968940/, (date accessed April 25, 2020).

Kaplan, R. S., and D. P. Norton. 2005. "The Balanced Scorecard: Measures that Drive Performance." *Harvard Business Review* 83, nos. 7/8, pp. 172–80.

Kaplan, R. S., and D. P. Norton. 2007. "Using the Balanced Scorecard as a Strategic Management System." *Harvard Business Review* 85, nos. 7/8, pp. 150–61.

Kapner, S. December 16, 2019. "It's Not You. Clothing Sizes Are Broken." *Wall Street Journal*. www.wsj.com/articles/its-not-you-clothing-sizes-are-broken-11576501384, (date accessed March 27, 2020).

Kim, S. H., M. A. Cohen, and S. Netessine. 2007. "Performance Contracting in After-Sales Service Supply Chains." *Management Science* 53, no. 12, pp. 1843–58.

Kim, S. H., M. A. Cohen, and S. Netessine. 2017. "Reliability or Inventory? An Analysis of Performance-Based Contracts for Product Support Services." In *Handbook of Information Exchange in Supply Chain Management*, eds. Albert Y. Ha and Christopher S. Tang 5, pp. 65–88.

Kimes, S. E., and J. E. Collier. 2015. "How Customers View Self-Service Technologies." *MIT Sloan Management Review* 57, no. 1, pp. 25–6.

Kinney, J. October 3, 2019. "Big Y Reintroduces Self-Service Kiosks at Western Mass. Supermarkets." *MassLive*. www.masslive.com/springfield/2019/10/big-y-reintroduces-self-service-kiosks-at-western-mass-supermarkets.html, (date accessed January 21, 2019).

Kickham, D. August 7, 2018. "Ritz-Carlton Guests are the Happiest, According to New Survey." *Forbes*. www.forbes.com/sites/debbikickham/2018/08/07/ritz-carlton-guests-are-the-happiest-according-to-new-survey/#100f38668e4f, (date accessed May 2, 2020 form).

Kiron, D., D. Palmer, A. N. Phillips, and N. Kruschwitz. 2012. "What Managers Really Think About Social Business." *MIT Sloan Management Review* 53, no. 4, pp. 51–60.

Ko, D. G., L. J. Kirsch, and W. R. King. 2005. "Antecedents of Knowledge Transfer from Consultants to Clients in Enterprise System Implementations." *MIS Quarterly* 29, no. 1, pp. 59–85.

Kowitt, B. September 6, 2010. "Insider Trader Joe's." *Fortune* 162, no. 4, pp. 86–96.

Kumar, V., and A. Pansari. 2015. "Measuring the Benefits of Employee Engagement." *MIT Sloan Management Review* 56, no. 4, pp. 67–72.

Kumar, A., and R. Telang. 2011. "Product Customization and Customer Service Costs: An Empirical Analysis." *Manufacturing & Service Operations Management* 13, no. 3, pp. 347–60.

Kuzela, C. June 30, 2015. "Smart Drugs: Where IoT Meets Healthcare, a Market Snapshot." *SiliconANGLE*. http://siliconangle.com/blog/2015/06/30/smart-drugs-where-iot-meets-healthcare-a-market-snapshot/, (date accessed June 22, 2016).

Latham, C. E., and G. Ling. July 1, 2019. "Social Robots Play Nicely with Others." *Scientific American.* www.scientificamerican.com/article/social-robots-play-nicely-with-others/, (date accessed April 13, 2020).

Lee, I., and Y.-J. Shin. 2020. "Machine Learning for Enterprises: Applications, Algorithm Selection, and Challenges." *Business Horizons* 63, pp. 157–70.

Leiber, N. March 29, 2020. "Curing Hospitals' Addiction to the Fossil Fuels that Make People Sick." *Boston Globe.* www.bostonglobe.com/2020/03/27/magazine/curing-hospitals-addiction-fossil-fuels-that-make-people-sick/, (date accessed May 2, 2020).

Li, M., T. Y. Choi, E. Rabinovich, and A. Crawford. 2013. "Self-Service Operations at Retail Stores: The Role of Inter-Customer Interactions." *Production and Operations Management* 22, no. 4, pp. 888–914.

Li, X.-B., X. Liu, and L. Motiwalla. 2020. "Valuing Personal Data with Privacy Consideration." *Decision Sciences Journal,* forthcoming, pp. 1–34.

Lock, M. January 2012a. *Data Management for BI: Big Data, Bigger Insight, Superior Performance.* Boston, MA: Aberdeen Group.

Lock, M. March 2012b. *Embedded BI: Boosting Analytical Adoption and Engagement.* Boston, MA: Aberdeen Group.

Looney, C. A., A. Y. Akbulut, and R. S. Poston. 2008. "Understanding the Determinants of Service Channel Preference in the Early Stages of Adoption: A Social Cognitive Perspective on Online Brokerage Services." *Decision Sciences* 39, no. 4, pp. 821–57.

Lowes. March 20, 2018. "Virtually View Lowe's Spring Collection in your Backyard." https://newsroom.lowes.com/fresh-thinking/virtually-view-lowes-spring-collection-in-your-backyard/, (date accessed April 7, 2020).

Lutz, A. 2013. "Costco Is Totally Eliminating Self-Checkout in Stores." *Business Insider,* June 6. www.businessinsider.com/costco-is-eliminating-self-checkout-2013-6, (date accessed April 25, 2020).

Lyons, D. 2012. "Cash Cloud." *Newsweek,* February 13, pp. 13–14.

MacDonald, I. January 14, 2014. "Hospitals Rank Alarm Fatigue as Top Patient Safety Concern." *FierceHealthcare.* www.fiercehealthcare.com/healthcare/hospitals-rank-alarm-fatigue-as-top-patient-safety-concern, (date accessed June 21, 2016).

Macy's. March 4, 2019. "Macy's Latest Collaborations and Technology Enhancements Are Set to Bring New Consumer Experiences to Its Best-in-Class App and In-Store." www.macysinc.com/investors/news-events/press-releases/detail/1549/macys-latest-collaborations-and-technology-enhancements, (date accessed April 7, 2020).

Malloy, D. March 20, 2020. "The Man Mapping Coronavirus with Smart Thermometers." *OZY*. www.ozy.com/the-new-and-the-next/the-man-mapping-coronavirus-with-smart-thermometers/290739/?utm_term=OZY&utm_source=Sailthru&utm_medium=email&utm_campaign=DailyDose%20%282020-03-23%2013:57:30%29&utm_content=Final, (date accessed April 14, 2020).

Malone, T. W., R. J. Laubacher, and T. Johns. 2011. "The Age of Hyperspecialization." *Harvard Business Review* 89, nos. 7/8, pp. 56–65.

Marcus, J. April 23, 2020. "Will the Coronavirus Forever Alter the College Experience?" *The New York Times*. www.nytimes.com/2020/04/23/education/learning/coronavirus-online-education-college.html, (date accessed April 27, 2020).

Marriott International 2019 Annual Report. https://marriott.gcs-web.com/static-files/b82978a6-9d28-4e38-9855-fc4ae2cebe11, (date accessed May 2, 2020).

Marvin, R. March 23, 2016. "5 Ways @WalmartLabs Is Revolutionizing Mobile Retail." *PC Magazine*. www.pcmag.com/article2/0,2817,2493418,00.asp, (date accessed April 25, 2020).

Mass.Gov. 2016. "Baker-Polito Administration Launches 'RMV Near Me' Program." https://blog.mass.gov/transportation/rmv/baker-polito-administration-launches-rmv-near-me-program/, (date accessed April 29, 2020).

McDougall, P. 2011. "Earthquake Fails to Halt NYSE Trading." *InformationWeek*, August 23. www.informationweek.com/earthquake-fails-to-halt-nyse-trading/d/d-id/1099740?, (date accessed April 25, 2020).

McGovern, M. November 27, 2017. "7 Reasons to Fire Customers, and How to Do It Right." *Customer Experience Insight*. http://www.customerexperienceinsight.com/7-reasons-to-fire-customers-and-how/, (date accessed April 17, 2020).

McKinsey & Company. 2020. www.mckinsey.com/solutions, (date accessed April 25, 2020).

Mehta, K. 2019. "Ahead of the Curve." *Quality Progress* 52, no. 10, pp. 30–9.

Merlo, O., A. B. Eisingerich, H.-K. Shin, and R. A. Britton. 2019. "Avoiding the Pitfalls of Customer Participation." *MIT Sloan Management Review* 61, no. 1, pp. 10–12.

Merrill, P. 2019. "Be Ready." *Quality Progress* 52, no. 10, pp. 54–6.

Metz, R. January 15, 2020. "There's a New Obstacle to Landing a Job after College: Getting Approved by AI." *CNN Business*. www.cnn.com/2020/01/15/tech/ai-job-interview/index.html, (date accessed April 6, 2020).

Meuter, M. L., M. J. Bitner, A. L. Ostrom, and S. W. Brown. 2005. "Choosing Among Alternative Service Delivery Modes: An Investigation of Customer Trial of Self-Service Technologies." *Journal of Marketing* 69, no. 2, pp. 61–83.

Miller, R. August 9, 2010. "NYSE Opens Mahwah Data Center." *Data Center Knowledge*. www.datacenterknowledge.com/archives/2010/08/09/nyse-opens-mahwah-data-center/, (date accessed April 25, 2020).

Montoya-Weiss, M. M., G. B. Voss, and D. Grewal. 2003. "Determinants of Online Channel Use and Overall Satisfaction with a Relational, Multichannel Service Provider." *Journal of the Academy of Marketing Science* 31, no. 4, pp. 448–58.

Morin, C. December 13, 2019. "How the Ritz-Carlton Creates a 5 Star Customer Experience." *CRM*. https://crm.org/articles/ritz-carlton-gold-standards, (date accessed May 2, 2010).

MTailor. 2020. www.mtailor.com, (date accessed March 29, 2020).

Muzaffar, M. March 30, 2020. "Can Coronavirus Make Online Dating Safer and Global – Permanently?" *OZY*. www.ozy.com/the-new-and-the-next/can-the-virus-make-online-dating-safer-and-global-permanently/291910/?utm_term=OZY&utm_source=Sailthru&utm_medium=email&utm_campaign=PDB%20%282020-03-31%2011:04:57%29, (date accessed March 31, 2020).

Nassauer, S. 2020. "Stores and Shoppers Agree: Self-Checkout is Hard." *Wall Street Journal*, February 13. www.wsj.com/articles/stores-and-shoppers-agree-self-checkout-is-hard-11581606705?mod=searchresults&page=1&pos=1, (date accessed February 17, 2020).

National Kidney Foundation. 2020. "Home Hemodialysis." www.kidney.org/atoz/content/homehemo, (date accessed May 12, 2020).

Oertzen, A.-S., G. Odekerken-Schröder, S. A. Brax, and B. Mager. 2018. "Co-creating Services: Conceptual Clarification, Forms and Outcomes. *Journal of Service Management* 29, no. 4, pp. 641–79.

Oliveira, P., and E. von Hippel. 2011. "Users as Service Innovators: The Case of Banking Services." *Research Policy* 40, no. 6, pp. 806–18.

Oracle. 2020. "Field Service Management." www.oracle.com/applications/customer-experience/service/field-service-management/, (date accessed April 25, 2020).

Ortho-Clinical Diagnostics. 2020. www.orthoclinicaldiagnostics.com/en-us/home/lab-reliability, (date accessed April 23, 2020).

"Outsourcing Is So Passé." 2012. *The Economist* 403, special section, pp. 8–9, June 2.

Parasuraman, A., V. A. Zeithaml, and L. Berry. 1988. "SERVQUAL: A Multiple-Item Scale for Measuring Consumer Perceptions of Service Quality." *Journal of Retailing* 64, no. 1, pp. 12–40.

Pietenpol, L. 2019. "Battling Bias." *Quality Progress* 52, no. 10, pp. 6–8.

PillPack. 2020. www.pillpack.com/, (date accessed April 25, 2020).

Predix. 2016. "What This Health Care Revolutions Means for You." *OZY*. www.ozy.com/the-new-and-the-next/what-this-health-care-revolution-means-for-you/70213/, (date accessed April 21, 2020).

Pollack, S. December 19, 2019. "MassDOT's Annual Performance Report." www.mass.gov/doc/2019-annual-performance-report/download, (date accessed April 29, 2020).

Postrel, V. August 13, 2015. "Robots Won't Rule the Checkout Lane." *Bloomberg View*. www.bloomberg.com/view/articles/2015-08-10/robots-won-t-rule-the-checkout-lane, (date accessed April 25, 2020).

"'Power by the Hour': Can Paying Only for Performance Redefine How Products Are Sold and Serviced?" February 21, 2007. *Knowledge @ Wharton*. http://knowledge.wharton.upenn.edu/article/power-by-the-hour-can-paying-only-for-performance-redefine-how-products-are-sold-and-serviced/, (date accessed April 25, 2020).

Pursuant Health. 2020. http://pursuanthealth.com/, (date accessed April 10, 2020).

Redman, R. June 18, 2019. "Albertsons to Deploy Self-Checkout Across Banners." *Supermarket News*. www.supermarketnews.com/retail-financial/albertsons-deploy-self-checkout-across-banners, (date accessed January 21, 2020).

Renzulli, K. A. March 20, 2020. "The Coronavirus Will Change How We Work Forever." *Newsweek*. www.newsweek.com/coronavirus-will-change-how-we-work-forever-1494854?utm_source=SilverpopMailing&utm_medium=email&utm_campaign=Work%20From%20Home%20One%20Off%20(1)&utm_content=, (date accessed March 30, 2020).

Retana, G. F., C. Forman, and D. J. Wu. 2016. "Proactive Customer Education, Customer Retention, and Demand for Technology Support: Evidence from a Field Experiment." *Manufacturing & Service Operations Management* 18, no. 1, pp. 34–50.

Roels, G. 2014. "Optimal Design of Coproductive Services: Interaction and Work Allocation." *Manufacturing & Service Operations Management* 16, no. 4, pp. 578–94.

Roose, K. December 12, 2018. "Is Tech Too Easy to Use?" *The New York Times*. www.nytimes.com/2018/12/12/technology/tech-friction-frictionless.html, (date accessed April 27, 2020).

Rust, R. T., and P. C. Verhoef. 2005. "Optimizing the Marketing Interventions Mix in Intermediate-Term CRM." *Marketing Science* 24, no. 3, pp. 477–89.

Rust, R. T., A. J. Zahorik, and T. L. Keiningham. 1995. "Return on Quality (ROQ): Making Service Quality Financially Accountable." *Journal of Marketing* 59, no. 2, pp. 58–70.

Ryan, T. June 17, 2019. "Does Self-Checkout Make Sense for Costco?" *Retail-Wire*. https://retailwire.com/discussion/does-self-checkout-make-sense-for-costco/, (date accessed January 21, 2020).

Sampson, S. E., and C. M. Froehle. 2006. "Foundations and Implications of a Proposed Unified Services Theory." *Production & Operations Management* 15, no. 2, pp. 329–43.

Sam's Club. 2020. "Skip the checkout line with Scan & Go." www .samsclub.com/content/scan-and-go, (date accessed January 21, 2020).

Schellmann, H. January 7, 2020. "How Job Interviews Will Transform in the Next Decade." *The Wall Street Journal.* www.wsj.com/articles/how-job-interviews-will-transform-in-the-next-decade-11578409136?shareToken=st 89e6c3228a3e496d8aa3464e440e5275&reflink=article_email_share, (date accessed April 9, 2020).

Schweer, M., D. Assimakopoulos, R. Cross, and R. J. Thomas. 2012. "Building a Well-Networked Organization." *MIT Sloan Management Review* 53, no. 2, pp. 35–42.

Shellenbarger, S. December 16, 2019. "Make Your Job Application Robot-Proof." *The Wall Street Journal.* www.wsj.com/articles/make-your-job-application-robot-proof-11576492201?shareToken=st7bb42049cbaa4571803c0c106f5 8ee70&reflink=article_email_share, (date accessed April 5, 2020).

Slack. 2020. https://slack.com/, (date accessed May 17, 2020).

Small Luxury Hotels of the World. 2020. www.slh.com, (date accessed March 29, 2020).

SoftBank Robotics. 2020. www.softbankrobotics.com/emea/en/pepper/, (date accessed April 13, 2020).

Starbucks. 2020. "Ethical Sourcing." www.starbucks.in/coffee/ethical-sourcing, (date accessed May 1, 2020).

Stone, Z. January 4, 2019. "Finding Your Inner Doctor: The Rise of New-Age DIY Tools." *OZY.* www.ozy.com/fast-forward/finding-your-inner-doctor-the-rise-of-new-age-diy-tools/91449/, (date accessed April 9, 2020).

Summers, N. November 28, 2011. "Bloomberg's Plan for World Domination." *Newsweek* 158, no. 22, pp. 44–9.

Swedberg, C. 2015. "Target Announces Nationwide RFID Rollout." *RFID Journal.* www.rfidjournal.com/articles/view?13060/, (date accessed June 21, 2016).

Sweeney, J. C., T. S. Danaher, and J. R. McColl-Kennedy. 2015. "Customer Effort in Value Cocreation Activities: Improving Quality of Life and Behavioral Intentions of Health Care Customers." *Journal of Service Research* 18, no. 3, pp. 318–35.

Szulanski, G. 2000. "The Process of Knowledge Transfer: A Diachronic Analysis of Stickiness." *Organizational Behavior and Human Decision Processes* 82, no. 1, pp. 9–27.

Tensator Group. October 14, 2013. "Tensator Survey Reveals Shoppers' Self-Service Frustration." www.tensatorgroup.com/tensator-survey-reveals-shoppers-self-service-frustration/, (date accessed June 19, 2016).

Terlep, S. August 3, 2019. "Everyone Hates Customer Service. This Is Why." *The Wall Street Journal.* www.wsj.com/articles/everyone-hates-customer-service-this-is-why-11564804882, (date accessed April 13, 2020).

Teva Pharmaceutical. 2020. www.proairdigihaler.com, (date accessed April 9, 2020).

TOA Technologies. November 2011. "2011 Cost of Waiting Survey: United States Results." http://toatech.com/costofwaiting/documents/TOA-Cost-of-Waiting-US_2011.pdf, (date accessed November 17, 2011).

Topol, E. J. January 9, 2015. "The Future of Medicine Is in Your Smartphone." *The Wall Street Journal.* www.wsj.com/articles/the-future-of-medicine-is-in-your-smartphone-1420828632, (date accessed April 25, 2020).

True Fit Website. 2020. www.truefit.com/, (date accessed March 27, 2020).

Uenlue, M. September 19, 2019. "Groupon Business Model Canvas." *Innovation Tactics.* https://innovationtactics.com/groupon-business-model-canvas/, (date accessed April 30, 2020).

Upton, D. M., and B. R. Staats. 2008. "Radically Simple IT." *Harvard Business Review* 86, no. 3, pp. 118–24.

Verhoef, P. C., A. T. Stephen, P. K. Kannan, X. Luo, V. Abhishek, M. Andrews, Y. Bart, et al. 2017. "Consumer Connectivity in a Complex, Technology-Enabled, and Mobile-Oriented World with Smart Products." *Journal of Interactive Marketing* 40, pp. 1–8.

Vilner, Y. July 20, 2018. "The Year of Blockchain and Sharing Economy's Intersection." *Forbes.* www.forbes.com/sites/yoavvilner/2018/07/20/the-year-of-blockchain-and-sharing-economys-intersection/#2e719aa14c28, (date accessed April 1, 2020).

VSee. 2020. www.vsee.com/messenger/, (date accessed April 12, 2020).

von Hippel, E. 1994. "'Sticky Information' and the Locus of Problem Solving: Implications for Innovation." *Management Science* 40, no. 4, pp. 429–39.

Waddock, S., and N. Smith. 2000. "Corporate Responsibility Audits: Doing Well by Doing Good." *Sloan Management Review* 41, no. 2, pp. 75–83.

Waldie, K. September 2011. *Beyond Logistics: Meeting Customer Needs for In-Home Services.* Sponsored by TOA Technologies. London: Economist Intelligence Unit Limited.

Wall Street Prep. 2020. "Bloomberg vs. Capital IQ vs. FactSet vs. Thomson Reuters Eikon." www.wallstreetprep.com/knowledge/bloomberg-vs-capital-iq-vs-factset-vs-thomson-reuters-eikon/, (date accessed March 30, 2020).

Weill, P., and S. L. Woerner. 2015. "Thriving in an Increasingly Digital Ecosystem." *MIT Sloan Management Review* 56, no. 4, pp. 27–34.

Weintraub, K. January 30, 2012. "Putting Care in Patients' Hands." *Boston Globe.* www.bostonglobe.com/business/2012/01/30/mit-media-lab-teams-compete-create-ways-patients-can-control-their-health/2Sne1Txbg1E 5hDon2Qh21H/story.html?s_campaign=8315, (date accessed May 11, 2020).

Wikipedia, Smart city. 2020. https://en.wikipedia.org/wiki/Smart_city, (date accessed April 14, 2020).

Wikipedia, Zoombombing. 2020. https://en.wikipedia.org/wiki/Zoombombing, (date accessed April 10, 2020).

Welch, D. July 15, 2016. "What Your Car Knows About You and Why Everyone Cares." *Boston Globe.* www.bostonglobe.com/lifestyle/2016/07/14/what-your-car-knows-about-you-and-why-everyone-cares/4TdG5n0X BFcdLXNF0IhcDM/story.html, (date accessed April 25, 2020).

Wolfinbarger, M., and M. C. Gilly. 2003. "eTailQ: Dimensionalizing, Measuring and Predicting Etail Quality." *Journal of Retailing* 79, no. 3, pp. 183–98.

Xue, M., and J. M. Field. 2008. "Service Co-production with Information Stickiness and Incomplete Contracts: Implications for Consulting Services Design." *Production and Operations Management* 17, no. 3, pp. 357–72.

Zipcar. 2020. https://support.zipcar.com/hc/en-us/articles/220675907-Zipcar-Fees-Fines, (date accessed April 17, 2020).

Zoom Blog. 2020. https://blog.zoom.us/wordpress/2020/04/01/a-message-to-our-users/, (date accessed April 10, 2020).

About the Author

Joy M. Field is an associate professor of operations management in the Carroll School of Management at Boston College. She received an MBA, an MS in statistics, and a PhD in operations management from the University of Minnesota. Her work has been published in leading journals such as the *Academy of Management Journal, Decision Sciences, Journal of Operations Management, Journal of Service Management, Production and Operations Management, and Strategic Management Journal.* She is an associate editor for *Decision Sciences, Journal of Service Management, and Journal of Service Research.*

Index

OTHER TITLES IN OUR SUPPLY AND OPERATIONS MANAGEMENT COLLECTION

Joy M. Field, Boston College, *Editor*

- *Operations Management in China* by Craig Seidelson
- *Logistics Management: An Analytics-Based Approach* by Tan Miller and Matthew J. Liberatore
- *The Practical Guide to Transforming Your Company* by Daniel Plung and Connie Krull
- *Leading and Managing Strategic Suppliers* by Richard Moxham
- *Moving the Chains: An Operational Solution for Embracing Complexity in the Digital Age* by Domenico LePore
- *The New Age Urban Transportation Systems, Volume I: Cases from Asian Economies* by Sundaravalli Narayanaswami
- *The New Age Urban Transportation Systems, Volume II: Cases from Asian Economies* by Sundaravalli Narayanaswami
- *Optimizing the Supply Chain* by Jay E. Fortenberry
- *Sustain: Extending Improvement in the Modern Enterprise* by W. Scott Culberson
- *Managing Using the Diamond Principle: Innovating to Effect Organizational Process Improvement* by Mark W. Johnson
- *Insightful Quality, Second Edition: Beyond Continuous Improvement* by Victor E. Sower and Frank K. Fair
- *The Global Supply Chain and Risk Management* by Stuart Rosenberg
- *Moving into the Express Lane: How to Rapidly Increase the Value of Your Business* by Rick Pay
- *The Effect of Supply Chain Management on Business Performance* by Milan Frankl
- *The High Cost of Low Prices: A Roadmap to Sustainable Prosperity* by David S. Jacoby
- *Sustainable Operations and Closed Loop Supply Chains, Second Edition* by Gilvan Souza

Concise and Applied Business Books

The Collection listed above is one of 30 business subject collections that Business Expert Press has grown to make BEP a premiere publisher of print and digital books. Our concise and applied books are for...

- Professionals and Practitioners
- Faculty who adopt our books for courses
- Librarians who know that BEP's Digital Libraries are a unique way to offer students ebooks to download, not restricted with any digital rights management
- Executive Training Course Leaders
- Business Seminar Organizers

Business Expert Press books are for anyone who needs to dig deeper on business ideas, goals, and solutions to everyday problems. Whether one print book, one ebook, or buying a digital library of 110 ebooks, we remain the affordable and smart way to be business smart. For more information, please visit **www.businessexpertpress.com**, or contact **sales@businessexpertpress.com**.